INSIGHT POC[K]

LONDON

Discovery CHANNEL

APA PUBLICATIONS
Part of the Langenscheidt Publishing Group

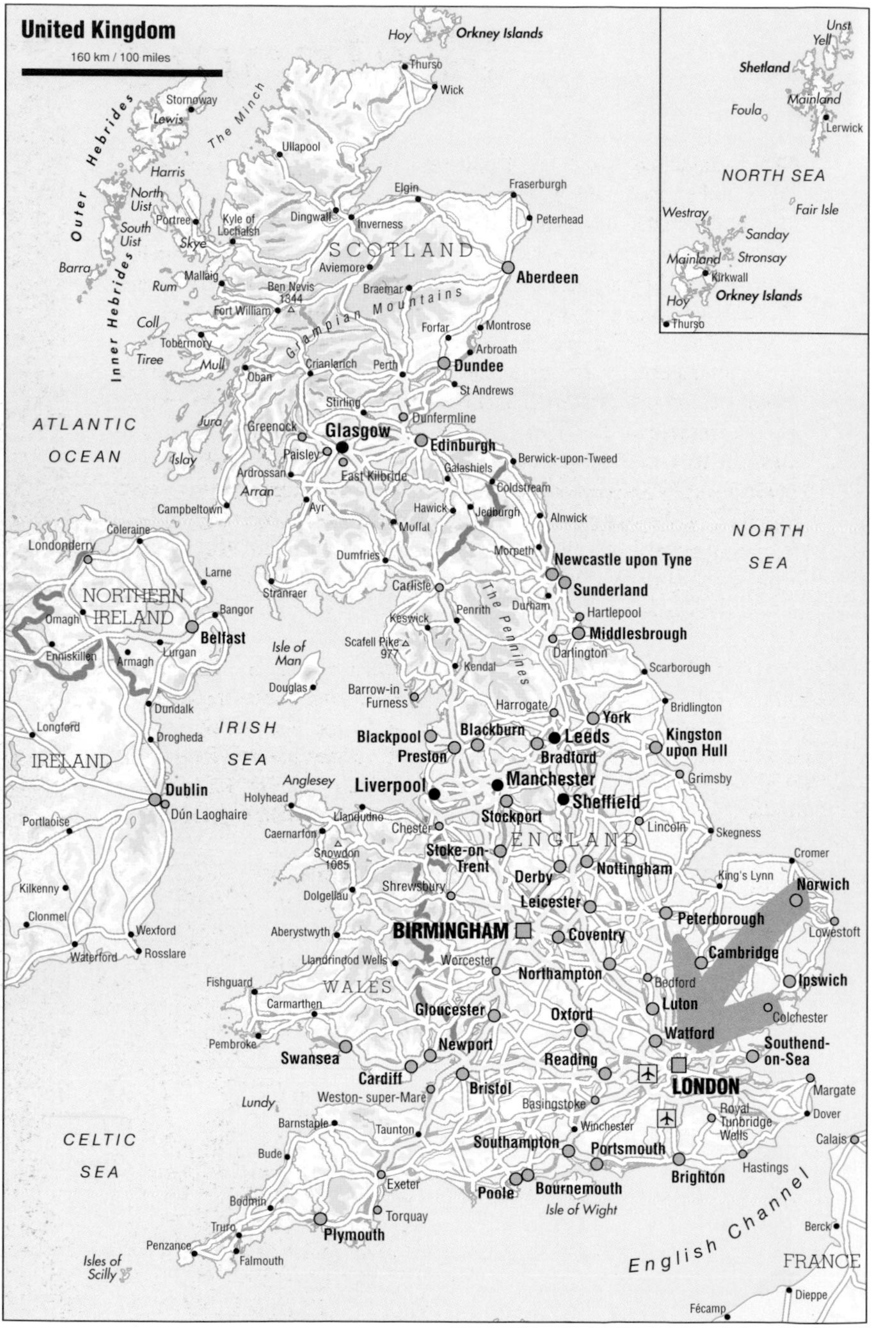
United Kingdom
160 km / 100 miles
Orkney Islands
Hoy
Thurso
Wick
Shetland
Unst
Yell
Foula
Mainland
Lerwick
NORTH SEA
Fair Isle
Westray
Sanday
Stronsay
Mainland
Kirkwall
Hoy
Orkney Islands
Thurso
Outer Hebrides
Stornoway
Lewis
The Minch
Harris
North Uist
South Uist
Barra
Inner Hebrides
Skye
Portree
Kyle of Lochalsh
Ullapool
Rum
Mallaig
Coll
Tobermory
Tiree
Mull
Oban
Fort William
Ben Nevis 1344
Dingwall
Inverness
Elgin
Fraserburgh
Peterhead
SCOTLAND
Aviemore
Aberdeen
Braemar
Grampian Mountains
Forfar
Montrose
Arbroath
Dundee
Crianlarich
Perth
St Andrews
Stirling
Dunfermline
Edinburgh
ATLANTIC OCEAN
Jura
Islay
Greenock
Glasgow
Paisley
East Kilbride
Ardrossan
Arran
Campbeltown
Ayr
Galashiels
Berwick-upon-Tweed
Coldstream
Hawick
Jedburgh
Alnwick
Moffat
Coleraine
Londonderry
Larne
NORTHERN IRELAND
Omagh
Enniskillen
Armagh
Lurgan
Bangor
Belfast
Dumfries
Stranraer
Carlisle
Morpeth
Newcastle upon Tyne
Sunderland
Durham
Hartlepool
Middlesbrough
Darlington
Penrith
Keswick
The Pennines
Scafell Pike 977
Isle of Man
Douglas
Kendal
Scarborough
Barrow-in-Furness
Bridlington
Dundalk
Longford
Drogheda
IRISH SEA
IRELAND
Harrogate
York
Blackpool
Blackburn
Leeds
Preston
Bradford
Kingston upon Hull
Grimsby
NORTH SEA
Dublin
Dún Laoghaire
Anglesey
Holyhead
Liverpool
Manchester
Sheffield
Stockport
Portlaoise
Caernarfon
Llandudno
Chester
Lincoln
Skegness
ENGLAND
Snowdon 1085
Stoke-on-Trent
Derby
Nottingham
Cromer
King's Lynn
Norwich
Kilkenny
Shrewsbury
Dolgellau
Leicester
Clonmel
Peterborough
Lowestoft
Wexford
Aberystwyth
BIRMINGHAM
Coventry
Waterford
Rosslare
Cambridge
Llandrindod Wells
Worcester
Northampton
Ipswich
Fishguard
WALES
Bedford
Luton
Colchester
Carmarthen
Gloucester
Oxford
Watford
Pembroke
Newport
Southend-on-Sea
Swansea
Reading
Cardiff
Bristol
LONDON
Margate
Lundy
Weston- super-Mare
Basingstoke
Royal Tunbridge Wells
Dover
Barnstaple
Winchester
Taunton
CELTIC SEA
Southampton
Portsmouth
Calais
Bude
Brighton
Hastings
Exeter
Poole
Bournemouth
Isle of Wight
Bodmin
Torquay
Plymouth
Truro
Penzance
Falmouth
Isles of Scilly
English Channel
Berck
FRANCE
Dieppe
Fécamp

Welcome

This guidebook combines the interests and enthusiasms of two of the world's best-known information providers: Insight Guides, who have set the standard for visual travel guides since 1970, and Discovery Channel, the world's premier source of non-fiction television programming. Its aim is to bring you London's top attractions in 17 tailor-made itineraries designed by two of Insight's best-informed correspondents.

From Wren's St Paul's to the Millennium Dome, from the formal Palace of Westminster to fashionable Notting Hill – though steeped in history, London is one of the fastest-changing and most exciting cities in the world, and rarely more so than during the first decade of the new millennium. It was in order to do full justice to both the historic and contemporary aspects of the city that Insight chose two writers from different generations to work on the guide. Together they present a fascinating metropolis. Whether this is your first visit, or your hundredth, you'll discover a city that is undergoing exciting renewal.

Roland Collins is a writer and historian, and has lived in the city for longer than he cares to remember. His main interest is in social history, but he is also an accomplished artist who exhibits in London. He says fondly of the city: 'We've been married for over 60 years. She isn't the girl I swapped vows with, but we are still very much in love.' This love shines through the walking tours he has put together.

Beverly Harper is also a massive enthusiast for everything to do with London, but especially the city's all-consuming passions: shopping, eating out and nightlife. Harper is well-schooled in both the trendy and the perennial in this great city, and she has selected something of both for you. We hope that her tips will help you to enjoy tasting, seeing and experiencing the essence of London.

SAMUEL JOHNSON

EXCURSIONS

LEISURE ACTIVITIES

CALENDAR OF EVENTS

PRACTICAL INFORMATION

MAPS

CREDITS AND INDEX

Pages 2/3: dolphin fountain by Tower Bridge
Pages 8/9: the ornate Houses of Parliament

CHE SARA SARA

History & Culture

Standing above the Thames on Tower Hill are the surprisingly substantial remains of Londinium, the city established 2,000 years ago by thrusting empire builders from southern Europe, the Romans. They imposed a civilisation where none existed before, lighting a lamp in the Celtic darkness.

In Trinity Square a section of the wall the Romans built to defend their city still dominates. Elsewhere the wall is threaded through the fabric of Victorian development or buried below modern street levels. As the capital of Britannia, as Roman Britain was called, London had its complement of imposing public buildings, and the excavated remains of the finest are on display at the Museum of London (see Walk 4: *Tower and City*).

Towards the end of the 3rd century London was beginning to be affected by instability and fighting overseas, which culminated in the withdrawal from Britain of the Roman garrison in 410 in the face of attacks elsewhere in the Empire by the Germanic hordes of northern Europe. The city's fabric crumbled, but London would rise again to importance under the Saxons.

For 200 years there is not a single written reference to London, until St Augustine was sent to establish a bishopric and the first St Paul's Cathedral was founded by Ethelbert. Little remains that mirrors Anglo-Saxon building skills, though there is ample evidence of their considerable craftsmanship in the Sutton Hoo ship burial in the British Museum.

In spite of an early defeat of the Danes by Alfred, King of Wessex, and his foresight in repairing the Roman walls, London eventually succumbed to the invaders. Sweyn, and later Canute, were crowned here in their palace at Aldermanbury. After the accession of Edward the Confessor in 1042 the Court moved to Westminster, and the rebuilding of the 10th-century abbey was begun. From then on kings were crowned, married and buried there.

William the Conqueror's defeat of the Saxons in 1066 heralded the introduction of a culture that was to transform a nation's art and architecture, literature and laws. William's building programme put priority on defence. His White Tower at the core of the Tower of London was completed by 1097, its monolithic bulk diminished since by walls and bastions. A new St Paul's was begun following a fire in 1097, and Westminster Hall in the Palace of Westminster was started 10 years later.

Bursting at the Seams

Under the Normans, London rapidly developed as a centre of trade and, over the next two centuries, the City of London evolved its characteristic pattern of narrow streets and alleys. Inside the walls crowded London's rapidly grow-

Left: bustling Covent Garden painted by Phoebus Leven (1864)
Right: Roman relic in the Museum of London

ing population: in the 12th century there were around 25,000 people, accommodated in timber-framed houses, worshipping in over 100 parish churches, and shopping in the Stocks Market where the Mansion House now stands, and in the great open-air market that was Cheapside.

One public building dating from the early 1400s survives – though it has been substantially patched, re-roofed and re-fronted – to remind us by its size and importance of the measures taken by the city's merchants to protect their trade interests: the Guildhall was the seat of city government and the principal meeting place of all those who wielded power in the city.

West of the City the legal profession meanwhile organised itself into Inns of Court – having something of the character of university colleges – in the Temple, Lincoln's Inn, Clifford's Inn and Gray's Inn. The Inns of Court probably had Geoffrey Chaucer as a student. By 1389 the author of *The Canterbury Tales* was Clerk of the King's Works in a city of approximately 50,000 inhabitants. The Black Death in 1348 succeeded where the authorities had failed in limiting the alarming rate of growth. Enforcement had proved ineffectual and by the mid-14th century London had grown well beyond the original walls.

Reading, Writing, Building

The spread of literacy echoed the swelling population. In 1476 a former apprentice to a London mercer, William Caxton, set up a press in Westminster, printing about 80 books, *The Canterbury Tales* and *Morte d'Arthur* among them. In Fleet Street Wynkyn de Worde printed the first book in English and unknowingly started the street's connection with the dissemination of popular culture through the newspaper.

In architecture, Henry VII had begun, at Westminster in 1503, the first complete chapel in the Late Perpendicular style, damned with faint praise by the great architect, Sir Christopher Wren, as 'embroidery' work. Henry's son Henry VIII brought much further-reaching changes to London: he set about demolishing the power of the Pope in England, which incidentally produced resources for his lavish private spending. The Dissolution of the Monasteries in 1536 brought him revenue and property. The city's monastic houses were soon replaced by private dwellings. A hospital gave way to St James's Palace; Charterhouse to a mansion for Lord North. Cardinal Wolsey's house became the nucleus of Whitehall Palace.

Above: medieval depiction of Charles d'Orléans' imprisonment in the Tower of London following his capture at Agincourt (1415), with the old London Bridge behind

England entered its 'Golden Age' with the accession of Queen Elizabeth I in 1558. If it was the greatest era in English history then it was the greatest in London's too, and one man, a Londoner by adoption, made an outstanding contribution – William Shakespeare. Banned from putting on his plays in the City, he joined another playwright, Ben Jonson, in setting up a playhouse on the less salubrious south bank of the river opposite St Paul's Cathedral, alongside bear pits and brothels. The thatch-topped theatres-in-the-round, the Hope, the Rose and the Globe, live on only in the names of streets and alleys on Bankside, but a replica of Shakespeare's Globe Theatre opened its doors in 1996.

Under Elizabeth I, London's first planning laws were introduced to discourage speculative building, as the population shot up from around 50,000 in 1530 to 225,000 by the end of the 16th century. The laws were not successfully enforced and former monastic lands and gardens became choked with shoddy tenements. If Elizabeth was a hard act to follow, her successor, James I, at least made an educated choice in Inigo Jones as his Surveyor to the King's Works. Jones, in his interpretations of the Italian architect Palladio's purity of style, brought a unique vision to his designs for the Queen's House at Greenwich. The Banqueting House in Whitehall, in which London was first introduced to Portland stone, and the Queen's Chapel in St James's remain to confirm the trail-blazing character of these major works. In Covent Garden he laid out the prototype of that typical urban feature, the London square, though this was savaged by the later intrusion of the market and the loss of its arcaded houses. St Paul's church still dominates the western side of the square.

Plague and Fire

In 1665 the Great Plague did what no amount of legislation had been able to achieve – it restricted London's population growth. One hundred thousand people died and were bundled into plague pits. A year later the City was ravaged by fire, destroying 13,200 houses, 87 parish churches, and the halls of 44 livery companies. Gothic St Paul's was so badly damaged as to make repair impossible.

Having fled to the countryside, wealthy former residents never returned to the City, and the drift to the westward suburbs grew as landowners like the Duke of Bedford made their estates available for development. However, the aldermen of the City of London accepted the challenge that renewal presented, and on Christopher Wren, Surveyor General to the Crown, fell the task of rebuilding. But Wren's imaginative scheme for Parisian-style boulevards, with a wide riverside quay replacing the huddle of wharves, was

Right: Queen Elizabeth I, who ruled from 1558–1603

abandoned in the face of strong demands for houses, shops and workshops.

So, the opportunity for redevelopment to a new plan having been lost, London rose again in the same street pattern. Yet, to the cathedral and parish churches, of which he rebuilt no less than 50, Wren brought an outstanding creativity. These churches, often on cramped or irregular sites – each one signalled by a tower or steeple, and each with its own unique personality – are the principal architectural glory of the City to this day, though their numbers have been decimated by destruction and disuse. St Paul's was started in 1675 and became Wren's acknowledged masterpiece, taking nearly 40 years to complete to parliament's satisfaction.

Meanwhile, speculative building was transforming the sites of the old mansions and private gardens between the Strand and the river, as well as Holborn, Soho, Mayfair and St James's. Only the railings of Hyde Park could halt the bricks and mortar joining London with the village of Kensington.

In the 18th century, London began to take on a new look characterised by the streets and squares in Bloomsbury and Mayfair. In the City, the Mansion House was built as an official residence for the Lord Mayor across from a Palladian home for the Bank of England. Whitehall had Government thrust upon it. The palace, deserted by the Court, was replaced with the public buildings which line it today. Barracks for the Horse Guards were followed by the Admiralty, where the Lords lived next to, if not over, the offices, and the Treasury moved to the site of the Tudor cockpit.

How the Other Half Lived

In 1801, at the first official count of heads, Londoners numbered nearly one million. These inhabitants were beginning to desert the City and crowd into Westminster and Holborn, St Marylebone and St Pancras, and across the river into Southwark, Lambeth and Bermondsey. London turned its back on the East End, which became the natural point of arrival for foreigners in flight from persecution. These newcomers brought their own skills and trades: the Huguenots brought silk weaving to Spitalfields; the Jews from Russia and Poland brought boot and shoe-making, clothing and furniture-making to the area east of Aldgate.

At the same time the construction of the docks swept away whole parishes. In 1825 St Katharine's Dock alone accounted for the loss of some 1,250 houses, displacing their inhabitants into neighbouring areas. The slums had come to London.

North and west London in the early 1800s showed the other side of the coin, reflecting the new prosperity in the spread of residential estates. Mansions and parkland yielded to their owners' realisation of the enhanced value that the needs of an expanding population was putting on their property. Perhaps the most significant of these developments centred on the Crown-owned lands of Marylebone Park. John Nash, the Prince Regent's architect, set out to create a garden city of villas and terrace houses for the rich in a Regent's Park connected by a triumphal way to the Prince's palace at Carlton House near Charing Cross. Compromise eventually reduced the promised 26 villas to eight and halved the circus to a single Park Crescent. Carlton House itself was demolished in favour of Carlton House Terrace.

London on the Move

Improved communications had exercised the minds of the authorities for some time, and they mainly focused on the river crossings. Waterloo, Southwark and Vauxhall bridges joined the existing bridges, Westminster and Blackfriars, in the early 19th century, and the medieval London Bridge was finally abandoned in favour of a new bridge, erected higher upstream, which was begun in 1831.

The unit of wheeled power was still the horse, and though the omnibus was bringing a new mobility to Londoners, a horse of a different metal was about to change the face of London. In 1841 the London and Blackwall Railway brought the first commuters to the City's Fenchurch Street. Most of the subsequent termini were not allowed so close to the centre, but the last miles of iron road through built-up areas were responsible for the loss of thousands of houses and created extensive slum areas.

The train sheds of the rail stations drew architects to the use of glass and iron. Paxton's palace of crystal for the Great International Exhibition of 1851 in Hyde Park was a natural step forward. His design, a doodle on a blotting pad, is as well known as a Leonardo cartoon. Here, the Victorians showed what Britain could make to over six million visitors, and took in over £400,000

Left: Regent Street was an integral part of John Nash's Grand Design for London
Above: the world's first underground railway system

at the turnstiles. Prince Albert, Queen Victoria's Consort, used the profits to build the Victoria and Albert Museum in South Kensington.

A fire that destroyed the old Palace of Westminster in 1834 provoked wholesale rebuilding on the site. The new Houses of Parliament might have looked very different, but of the two styles on offer to the competing architects, Elizabethan or Gothic, Charles Barry, with Pugin's help, won approval for his astonishing tour de force. Gothic was the flavour of the age. By 1847 the House of Lords was completed, followed by the Commons and Big Ben in 1858 and the Victoria Tower two years later. Familiar landmarks and streetscapes were dropping into place. Victorian by-passes like the Embankment, Victoria Street and Chelsea Embankment liberated congested streets. Shaftesbury Avenue and New Oxford Street cut swathes through the 'rookeries' of St Giles. 'Dwellings' began to appear as philanthropists such as the American George Peabody tackled the shame of London's poor, and a new London County Council took on the problems of a city expanded out of all proportion, problems which were to be compounded by the horrendous damage of war during the 20th century.

Post-War London

The Blitz left huge areas of the East End, most of its population evacuated to the countryside, in ruins. An opportunity for imaginative rebuilding was lost. Many of the faceless tower blocks and offices that were built in the 1950s and 1960s in the gaps created by the bombs are now themselves coming down. In their place, new and innovative buildings are transforming London's skyline. Since the 1980s, the Docklands have undergone a transformation, with the building of office blocks (Canary Wharf is London's tallest edifice) and 'yuppie' flats. Even the 'square mile' of the original City, hub of the nation's business community and regarded as conservative, is not immune to change – as anyone who has seen Richard Rogers's controversial Lloyd's Building (see Walk 4: *Tower and City*) will agree.

Thanks to substantial funding from the country's new National Lottery and a desire to mark the millennium, the late 1990s saw a massive injection of money into grand public projects , including, for example, the revamped Royal Opera House, the new Tate Gallery of Modern Art, and downriver in Greenwich, the Millennium Dome. The London of today has a buzz of self-confident optimism that it has lacked for decades. All it needs is someone to look after it – and Londoners hope that their new mayor, elected by popular mandate in the year 2000, will fulfil the role.

Above: the interior of the Lloyd's Building

History Highlights

43AD Romans found Londinium.
60 London set on fire and destroyed by Boadicea.
1065 Westminster Abbey consecrated by Edward the Confessor.
1066 William the Conqueror crowned in Westminster Abbey.
1097 Completion of the Tower of London's White Tower.
1190 London's first mayor.
1215 Magna Carta signed.
1265 First English Parliament.
1269 Present Westminster Abbey is consecrated.
1348 Start of the Black Death; 60,000 – half London's population – die.
1476 Caxton's first printing press set up at Westminster.
1509 Henry VIII builds St James's Palace.
1536 Henry instigates the Dissolution of the Monasteries.
1558 Accession of Elizabeth I.
1585 William Shakespeare arrives in London.
1598 Globe Theatre built.
1605 Guy Fawkes fails to blow up the Houses of Parliament.
1625 Inigo Jones completes the Banqueting House.
1631 Covent Garden laid out.
1635 Inigo Jones's Queen's House, Greenwich (now the Maritime Museum) is completed.
1649 Charles I is executed at the Banqueting House.
1660 Restoration of the monarchy; Charles II becomes king.
1665 The Great Plague; a total of 100,000 people die.
1666 The Great Fire of London; half the city is destroyed.
1666–1723 Christopher Wren rebuilds St Paul's and 51 other London churches.
1806 Nelson buried in St Paul's.
1815 John Nash lays out Regent's Park, Regent Street and The Mall.
1824 National Gallery founded.
1829 First London police force and London bus (horse drawn).
1835 Building work begins on the Houses of Parliament.
1836 London's first passenger railway opens for business.
1837 Accession of Queen Victoria; Buckingham Palace becomes the Sovereign's official residence.
1843 Nelson's Column erected.
1847 British Museum completed.
1851 The Great Exhibition takes place in Hyde Park.
1863 London's first underground railway line opens.
1894 Tower Bridge is completed.
1905 Harrods' present shop opens.
1914–18 World War I.
1926 The General Strike.
1939–45 World War II; the Blitz destroys much of the City and East End.
1951 Festival of Britain; the Festival Hall opens.
1952 Accession of Elizabeth II.
1956 Passing of the Clean Air Act.
1973 New London Bridge opens.
1976 National Theatre opens.
1986 Greater London Council is abolished.
1991 Canary Wharf, London's tallest building, completed in the restored Docklands area.
1994 The Channel Tunnel links London with Brussels and Paris.
1996 A replica of Shakespeare's Globe Theatre opens at Bankside.
1997 The funeral of Diana, Princess of Wales, brings thousands of mourners on to the streets of London.
1999 The Millennium Dome opens in Greenwich.
2000 The new London mayor is elected.

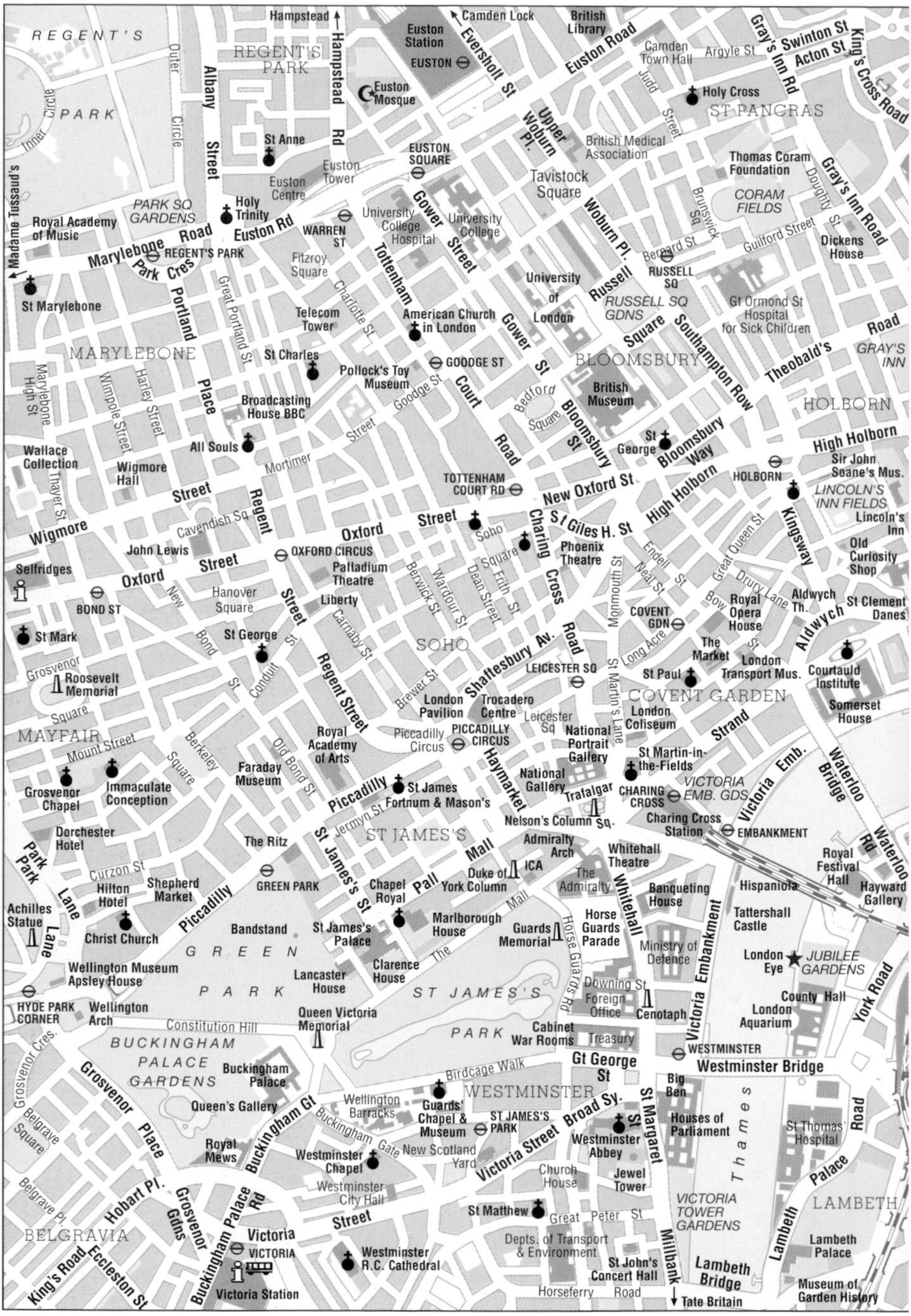
REGENT'S PARK
Hampstead
Camden Lock
British Library
Euston Station
EUSTON
Eversholt St
Euston Road
Camden Town Hall
Argyle St
Gray's Inn Rd
Swinton St
Acton St
King's Cross Road
REGENT'S PARK
Outer Circle
Albany Street
Hampstead Rd
Euston Mosque
Upper Woburn Pl.
Judd Street
Holy Cross
ST PANCRAS
Inner Circle
St Anne
British Medical Association
EUSTON SQUARE
Euston Tower
Euston Centre
Tavistock Square
Thomas Coram Foundation
Doughty St
Gray's Inn Road
Madame Tussaud's
PARK SQ GARDENS
Holy Trinity
University College Hospital
University College
Gower Street
Woburn Pl.
Brunswick Sq
CORAM FIELDS
Royal Academy of Music
Euston Rd
WARREN ST
Bernard St
Guilford Street
Dickens House
Marylebone Road
REGENT'S PARK
Park Cres
Fitzroy Square
Tottenham
RUSSELL SQ
Russell
University of London
RUSSELL SQ GDNS
Gt Ormond St Hospital for Sick Children
St Marylebone
Great Portland St
Charlotte St
Telecom Tower
American Church in London
Gower St
Square
Southampton Row
Theobald's Road
Portland
MARYLEBONE
St Charles
GOODGE ST
BLOOMSBURY
GRAY'S INN
Marylebone High St
Wimpole Street
Harley Street
Place
Pollock's Toy Museum
Goodge St
Court Road
Bedford Square
British Museum
HOLBORN
Broadcasting House BBC
Street
Bloomsbury St
All Souls
St George
Bloomsbury Way
High Holborn
Wallace Collection
Wigmore Hall
Mortimer
TOTTENHAM COURT RD
HOLBORN
Sir John Soane's Mus.
Thayer St
Street
Regent
New Oxford St
High Holborn
LINCOLN'S INN FIELDS
Cavendish Sq
Oxford
Street
Charing
St Giles H. St
Kingsway
Lincoln's Inn
Wigmore
John Lewis
OXFORD CIRCUS
Soho Square
Phoenix Theatre
Monmouth St
Endell St
Great Queen St
Old Curiosity Shop
Selfridges
Oxford
Street
Palladium Theatre
Berwick St
Wardour St
Dean Street
Frith St
Cross
Neal St
Drury Lane
BOND ST
New
Hanover Square
Street
Liberty
Road
COVENT GDN
Bow St
Royal Opera House
Aldwych Th.
St Clement Danes
Bond
Carnaby St
SOHO
Long Acre
Aldwych
St Mark
St George
Shaftesbury Av.
The Market
London Transport Mus.
Grosvenor
Roosevelt Memorial
St
Conduit St
Regent Street
LEICESTER SQ
St Martin's Lane
St Paul
Courtauld Institute
Brewer St
London Pavilion
Trocadero Centre
COVENT GARDEN
Square
Leicester Sq
London Coliseum
Somerset House
MAYFAIR
Berkeley
Old Bond St
Royal Academy of Arts
Piccadilly Circus
PICCADILLY CIRCUS
National Portrait Gallery
Strand
Mount Street
Square
Faraday Museum
Haymarket
St Martin-in-the-Fields
Waterloo Bridge
Grosvenor Chapel
Immaculate Conception
Piccadilly
St James
Fortnum & Mason's
National Gallery
Trafalgar
VICTORIA EMB. GDS
CHARING CROSS
Victoria Emb.
Jermyn St
Nelson's Column
Sq.
Charing Cross Station
EMBANKMENT
Dorchester Hotel
The Ritz
ST JAMES'S
Admiralty Arch
Whitehall Theatre
Waterloo Rd
Park
Curzon St
St James's St
Mall
Royal Festival Hall
Hilton Hotel
Shepherd Market
GREEN PARK
Pall
Duke of York Column
ICA
The Admiralty
Banqueting House
Hispaniola
Hayward Gallery
Lane
Chapel Royal
Mall
Achilles Statue
Christ Church
Piccadilly
Marlborough House
Horse Guards Parade
Whitehall
Tattershall Castle
Bandstand
St James's Palace
Guards Memorial
Horse Guards Rd
Ministry of Defence
London Eye
JUBILEE GARDENS
GREEN PARK
The
Lane
Wellington Museum Apsley House
Clarence House
Lancaster House
Victoria Embankment
County Hall
York Road
HYDE PARK CORNER
Wellington Arch
ST JAMES'S PARK
Downing St
Foreign Office
Cenotaph
London Aquarium
Constitution Hill
Queen Victoria Memorial
Cabinet War Rooms
Treasury
BUCKINGHAM PALACE GARDENS
WESTMINSTER
Westminster Bridge
Grosvenor Cres.
Grosvenor
Buckingham Palace
Birdcage Walk
Gt George St
Big Ben
Belgrave Square
Place
Queen's Gallery
Buckingham Gt
Wellington Barracks
WESTMINSTER
Guards' Chapel & Museum
ST JAMES'S PARK
Broad Sy.
St Margaret St
Houses of Parliament
Thames
St Thomas' Hospital
Road
Royal Mews
Buckingham Gate
New Scotland Yard
Victoria Street
Westminster Abbey
Westminster Chapel
Jewel Tower
Palace
Belgrave Pl.
Hobart Pl.
Grosvenor Gdns
Buckingham Palace Rd
Westminster City Hall
Church House
VICTORIA TOWER GARDENS
LAMBETH
St Matthew
Great Peter St
Street
Millbank
Lambeth
BELGRAVIA
Victoria
VICTORIA
Depts. of Transport & Environment
Westminster R.C. Cathedral
St John's Concert Hall
Lambeth Bridge
Lambeth Palace
King's Road
Eccleston St
Victoria Station
Horseferry Road
Tate Britain
Museum of Garden History

London
500 m / 550 yds
Sadler's Wells
Rosebery Av.
St John St
Goswell Road
City Road
St Clement
The City University
Lever Street
Moorfields Eye Hospital
Bath Street
Vestry St
East Rd
City Rd
City & East London College
Fitfield Street
OLD STREET
Old St
Curtain Rd
FINSBURY
Percival St
Skinner St
Farringdon Rd
Mount Pleasant Sorting Office
CLERKENWELL
Rosebery Av.
St John St
Goswell Rd
Old Street
Great Eastern Street
Shoreditch High Street
Bethnal Gn Rd
City Road
ST LUKE'S
Clerkenwell Rd
Old Street
Bunhill Row
Honourable Artillery Co.
BUNHILL FIELDS
Commercial St
Clerkenwell Rd
Museum of the Order of St John
St Bartholomew's Medical School
Exhibition Halls
City University
Chiswell St
Gray's Inn Rd
Leather Lane
Hatton Garden
Farringdon Rd
FARRINGDON STATION
Charterhouse
BARBICAN
Aldersgate Street
Beech St
Arts Centre
Finsbury Pavement
BROADGATE
Norton Folgate
SPITALFIELDS
Gray's Inn
Charterhouse St
Smithfield Market
Barbican Station
The Barbican
Liverpool Street Station
CHANCERY LA.
St Bartholomew the Great
Moorgate Station
MOORGATE
Broadgate
Bishopsgate
Museum of London
Finsbury Circus
LIVERPOOL ST
Middlesex Street
Whitechapel Art Gallery
Holborn
Holborn Circus
St Bartholomew's Hospital
London Wall
Moorgate
Petticoat Lane Market
Staple Inn
St Andrew
London Wall
Holborn Viaduct
Guildhall
Chancery Lane
Fetter Lane
City Thameslink Station
Newgate St
National Postal Mus.
Gresham Street
THE CITY
Nat. West Tower
Houndsditch
Bishopsgate
Dr Johnson's House
Old Bailey
ST PAUL'S
Stock Ex.
St Helen
Dukes Pl
Baltic Exchange
Royal Courts of Justice
Fleet Street
Ludgate Circus
St Paul's Cathedral
Bank of England (Extension)
St Mary-le-Bow
Bank of England
Threadneedle St
ALDGATE
Strand
St Bride's (Crypt Museum)
New Bridge St
St Paul's Churchyd
Queen Street
Royal Ex.
Leadenhall St
Lloyd's
Inner Temple Hall
BLACKFRIARS
College of Arms
Queen Victoria St
BANK
Lombard St
Gracechurch St
Leadenhall
Minories
Middle Temple
On Victoria St
Mansion House
King William St
Fenchurch St
Fenchurch St Station
Inner Temple
Queen Victoria St
MANSION HOUSE
CANNON ST
Cannon St
St Katharine's Docks
TEMPLE
Victoria Embankment
Blackfriars Station
Upp. Thames St
MONUMENT
Eastcheap
Great Tower St
Trinity House
TOWER HILL
The Monument
Byward St
Tower Hill
H.Q.S. Wellington
H.M.S. President
Blackfriars Bridge
Millennium Bridge
Southwark Bridge
Cannon St Station
Fish St Hill
Lower Thames St
Custom House
The Tower of London
Globe Theatre
London Bridge
Thames
Nat. Film Theatre
Gabriel's Wharf
Oxo Tower
Tate Modern Gallery
Clink St Exhibition
Royal National Theatre
Stamford Street
Blackfriars Road
Southwark Bridge Road
Southwark Cathedral
Hay's Galleria
H.M.S. Belfast
Tower Bridge
Christ Church
Southwark Street
Duke St Hill
Southwark Crown Court
BFI London IMAX Cinema
Waterloo East Station
SOUTHWARK
Southwark St
LONDON BRIDGE
London Dungeon
Tooley Street
St John
SOUTHWARK
Borough High Street
St Thomas Street
London Bridge Station
Design Museum
WATERLOO
Union Street
Union St
Guy's Hospital
Bridge Rd
Young Vic Theatre
The Cut
St Andrew with St Thomas
Waterloo Station & International Rail Terminal
The Old Vic Theatre
Marshalsea Rd
St George the Martyr
Bermondsey Street
Jamaica Rd
BOROUGH
St Hugh
Druid Street
Waterloo Road
Blackfriars Road
Southwark Bridge Road
Borough High St
Long Lane
Tower Bridge Rd
Baylis Rd
LAMBETH NORTH
Westminster Bridge Road
Borough Road
Harper Road
Great Dover Street
St Mary Magdalen
Kennington Road
South Bank University
Southwark Cwy
Trinity Church
BERMONDSEY
St George's Cathedral
St George's Road
London Rd
Newington
NEWINGTON
Grange Road
Lambeth
Imperial War Museum
ELEPHANT & CASTLE
Harper Road
Tower Bridge Road
London College of Printing
Elephant & Castle Station
New Kent Road

BOOKS etc.
BOOKS

City Itineraries

London is a city that you can only really get to know by walking the streets. The first six walks in this guide show you the major sights that every visitor comes to see. The next seven are designed for visitors with time to explore further areas and aspects of the city, and they show you some of the author's favourite London districts. The excursions section takes you by way of the Thames to the museums and royal palaces at Greenwich and Hampton Court, to Kew Gardens, and lastly to Hampstead, arguably London's most pleasing and leafiest suburb.

1. Covent Garden and Soho *(see map, page 22)*

A day spent exploring the Covent Garden area, with its buskers, shops and quality restaurants, and both seedy and chic Soho, home to London's Chinatown. The day ends at Leicester Square.

Start at Tottenham Court Road Station (Northern and Central Tube lines)

Walk away from the unmissable skyscaper Centrepoint, and head down St Giles High Street for the serenity of **St Giles in the Fields**. Henry Flitcroft's rebuilding of the church in the 1730s mirrors the work of Wren and Gibbs at St Martin-in-the-Fields, and the decoration of the interior in subtle tints of colour and gilt is exquisitely done. Look for the monument to George Chapman, translator of Homer. It was designed by his friend Inigo Jones.

Imagine yourself manacled, in a cart, on your way to be hanged at Tyburn Tree. **The Angel**, the ordinary enough pub next to the church, is where you would have had your last pint. This was the last inn on the country lane that led to the gallows at Marble Arch.

Continue to the junction with Shaftesbury Avenue. Pedestrianised **Neal Street**, opposite you on the right, has all the flavour of Covent Garden's new image in its shops and craft workshops – Eastern instruments, natural shoes, baskets and kites, laced with restaurants biased to lentils and yoghurt. This is the London of the trendy, the young and the beautiful. First right in Shorts Gardens is the entrance to **Neal's Yard**, a cornucopia of grains, dried fruit, cereals and peanut butter, their heady aromas mixing with the smell of freshly baked bread. There's healthy eating here, as well as walk-in massage, aromatherapy – or any therapy you want. Look out for the fabulous cheese shop just beyond the yard. Also on Shorts Gardens, notice the eccentric and entertaining water-driven sculpture that functions as a clock above the wholefood warehouse window. Behind you here is the

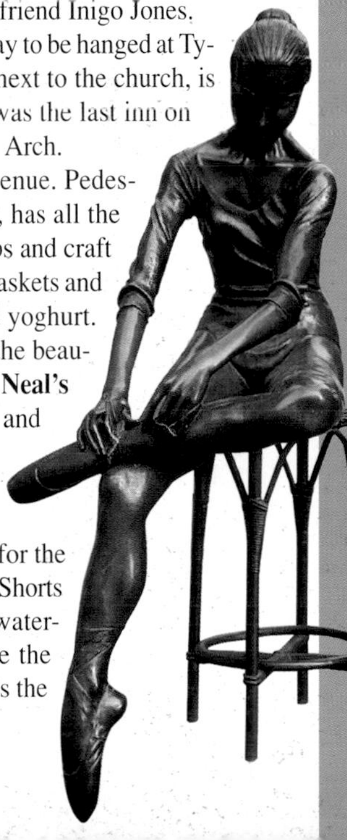

Left: performance art is everywhere in Covent Garden
Right: seated outside the Royal Opera House

entrance to a shopping centre, **Thomas Neal's**, with exclusive but alternative shops full of interesting ideas in an elegant glass-house setting.

Continue down Neal Street to the end – passing **Neal Street East** on your right, a warehouse of Asian arts – then nip across Long Acre and into James Street, with the market just ahead. But first go left into Floral Street and right on Bow Street, home of the 'Bow Street Runners', the forerunners of the police. Opposite the police station is the giant, imposing **Royal Opera House**, which reopened at the end of 1999 after a costly two-year overhaul.

Haunted Theatre

Russell Street leads left to the **Theatre Royal Drury Lane**, like the Opera House vulnerable to fire and the fourth theatre on this site since 1663. With many Georgian features, the ghost-haunted theatre has seen a procession of great names – Garrick, Sheridan, Kean, Sarah Siddons and Nell Gwynne, the local girl who sold oranges on opening nights, became an actress, and won a king's heart.

Don't feel you must dress up for the **Theatre Museum** (Tues–Sun 10am–6pm) in Russell Street. This beautifully mounted tribute to the per-

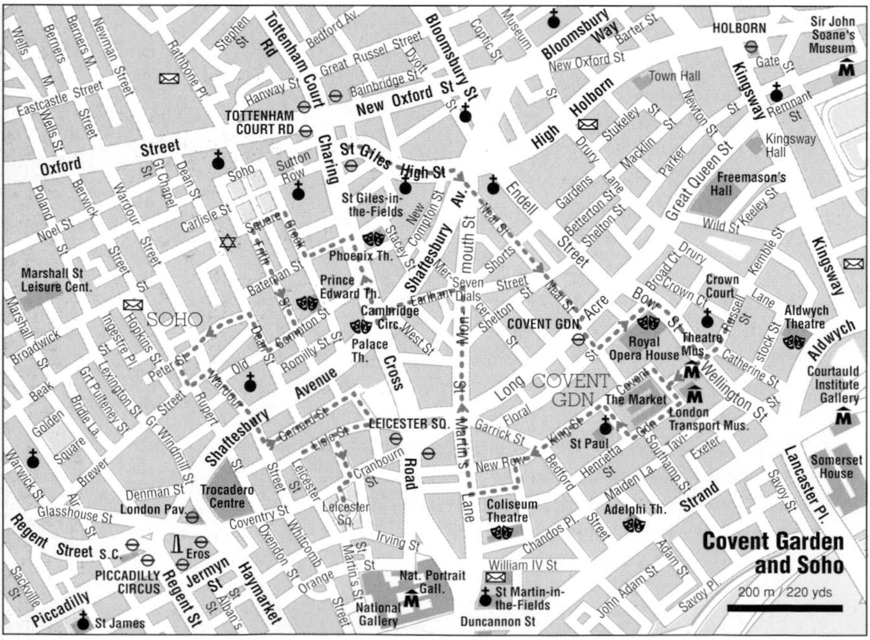

forming arts gives you a seat in the stalls for a thousand performances of musical comedy and melodrama, circus and panto, all for the price of one seat in the gallery. Just round the corner on Covent Garden is the **Transport Museum** (daily 10am–6pm, Friday 11am–6pm). How did ladies preserve their modesty on the knifeboard omnibus?

The market fills **Covent Garden**, London's first square, whose name derives from its original function as the Convent Garden of Westminster Abbey. In the 1630s the fourth Earl of Bedford had the imagination to ask Inigo Jones to lay out a new residential estate. Houses in the terraces facing the square were set above arcades as in the Rue de Rivoli in Paris, but the only vestige of the 'Great Piazza' remaining is a recreated portion on the north side. The Duke later exploited the garden as a vegetable market, frightening off respectable tenants, and fathering the produce market which moved to Nine Elms in 1974.

In the centre of Covent Garden is the **Apple Market** (Mon: antiques; Tues–Sun: arts and crafts), given over to a variety of British craftspeople, and surrounding it are speciality shops like Pollock's, home of the toy theatre and the 'Penny Plain, Twopence Coloured' prints that have fascinated lovers of the theatre for generations. **The Punch & Judy** pub is a reminder that nearby Punch's Puppet Show was first performed in England. Samuel Pepys, the 17th-century London diarist, was there.

The Handsomest Barn

Whatever the weather, you can enjoy eating outside here, thanks to the glass canopies, and watch the entertainment provided by the buskers. What finer backdrop could they have than the canopied front of **St Paul's church**? This is the rear of 'the handsomest barn in England', Inigo Jones's neat compromise to conform with the layout of the square. The church's entrance is through an arched passage off King Street. Thespians have made St Paul's their Valhalla; Prima Ballerina Tamara Karsavina, Donald Wolfit, Charles Chaplin and Noel Coward are remembered on the walls.

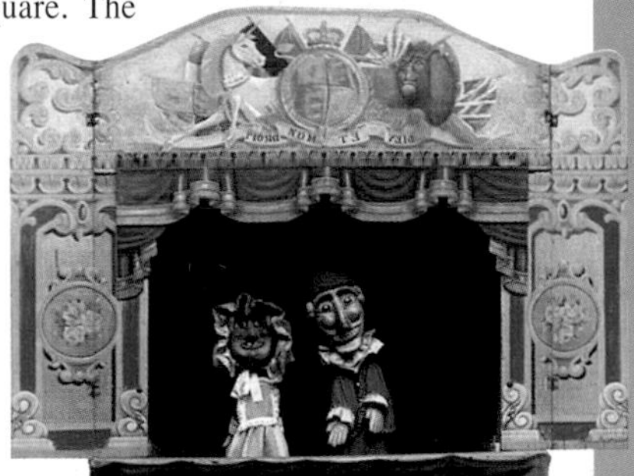

Go down King Street and cross into the pedestrianised New Row. Turn left into Bedfordbury and enter Goodwin's Court, which has a tiny entrance just 20 yards/metres from the corner. Walk down the alley past picturesque bow fronts. Cross St Martin's Lane to the **Salisbury**, for a drink at the marble-topped bar amid the dazzle of cut glass, mirrors and Art Nouveau lights.

For an upmarket fish lunch see if you can get a table at **Sheekey's** in St Martin's Court, or much less expensively have a simple sandwich or salad at a branch of the sandwich chain **Prêt à Manger** on the corner of Cranbourn Street. For a leisurely after-lunch browse, try Cecil Court's bookshops, or take in the **Photographers' Gallery** on Great Newport Street (Mon–Sat, 11am–6pm, Sun noon–6pm).

Above left: flower seller dressed for the part in Covent Garden's Apple Market
Right: Punch's Puppet Show

Soho's Microcosm

Continue up Monmouth Street to **Seven Dials** and the renewed obelisk. One of the seven sundials faces down Earlham Street, a microcosm of an earlier London, with street stalls, a butcher called Portwine, and Collins the ironmonger. At Cambridge Circus turn right up Charing Cross Road to **Foyle's**, once the world's largest bookshop, and left into Manette Street, which owes its name to Dickens's Dr Manette in *A Tale of Two Cities*. This is a fitting introduction to Soho, where French émigrés found refuge from the Revolution. Soho was seedy London, but trendy bars and shops have moved in.

Turn right into Greek Street to **Soho Square**. Most of its 18th-century houses have been surrendered to commerce, but No 1 Greek Street has enjoyed a charmed life thanks to the **House of Charity**. Although only open for a couple of hours two days a week (Wed 2.30–4.15pm, Thurs 11am–12.30pm), the magnificent staircase and plasterwork can just be glimpsed from the street. A statue of Charles II shares the square's garden with a ventilation shaft heavily disguised as a half-timbered cottage. At No 6 Frith Street, just south of the square, William Hazlitt, the critic and essayist, breathed his last words, 'Well, I've had a happy life,' which should please visitors to Hazlitt's, the hotel. Celebrities often stay here.

At the bottom of Frith Street you can stop for an *espresso* boost in one of several Italian cafés, such as **Bar Italia**, or a French pastry round the corner at **Valerie** on Old Compton Street. Off Dean Street, where Karl Marx wrote *Das Kapital*, Meard Street leads to Peter Street and **Berwick Market**, London's best open-air fruit and vegetable market. Squeeze through Walker's Court to the comparative calm of **Rupert Street**, with more stalls, choicer goods and higher prices. From Brewer Street turn right into Wardour Street, home to Britain's film industry. On the left is the tower of **St Anne's** church, with its 'beer barrel' spire.

Cross Shaftesbury Avenue on Wardour Street and turn left into pedestrian Gerrard Street, better known as **Chinatown**, where the street signs are in Chinese as well as English, and the open gates make it a welcoming yet foreign place. Turn right at the end into Newport Place and right again into Lisle Street. Between here and Leicester Square, on Leicester Place, is the French church, **Notre Dame de France**, and in the peace of its side chapel, a mural by Jean Cocteau. **Leicester Square**, with the Swiss Centre's performing clock and the city's major first-run cinemas, is a popular meeting place, especially in the evenings, when it heaves with people.

Above: Leicester Square's Empire

2. ROYAL PROGRESS *(see map, page 27)*

From Trafalgar Square to Whitehall, in time to see the Changing of the Guard; through leafy St James's Park to the royal residences of the Queen Mother (St James's Palace) and the Queen (Buckingham Palace).

Start at Charing Cross Station (Bakerloo, Jubilee, Northern Tube lines)

Thank heaven for the royals. So much of the history and character of London has been shaped by kings and queens, either by intent or default, that we owe them this tribute for the distinguished and beautiful buildings and the green and pleasant places that link them.

'If it's good enough for Nelson, it's quite good enough for me,' runs the old music hall song. **Trafalgar Square** has always been a people's place, the home of demonstrations and freedom of speech, yet its royal associations make it a good starting point. From the portico of the **National Gallery**, the country's foremost collection of pre-20th century art (daily 10am–6pm, except Wed 10am–9pm) you get a good view at bus-top level. Here was the Royal Mews when the Prince Regent, later George IV, had his residence at Carlton House nearby. The columns, which frame **Nelson's Column**, London's most famous statue, and, more distantly, St Stephen's Tower, were re-used when the gallery was built in 1838. The Sainsbury Wing, added in 1991, earned royal approval from the Prince of Wales. Tucked behind the National Gallery on Charing Cross Road is the **National Portrait Gallery** (Mon–Sat 10am–6pm, Sun noon–6pm), full of famous faces. These galleries could fill the best part of a day, but don't lose track of the time if you want to catch the Changing of the Guard in Whitehall at 11am.

In Trafalgar Square's northeast corner George IV sits astride a horse without a saddle, boots or stirrups. James II by Grinling Gibbons, on the lawn in front of the National Gallery, fares little better. Hand on hip, he is inexplicably dressed as an ancient Roman.

Above: Trafalgar Square and the National Gallery
Right: Nelson's Column

When **St Martin-in-the-Fields**, which overlooks the square, was completed in 1726, one parishioner, who had already paid for nearly half the cost, gave the workmen a 100-guinea bonus; that benefactor was George III and the architect was James Gibbs. St Martin's has the royal arms over the portico as well as over the chancel arch, and royalty sits in London's only royal pew. Charles II was baptised here, and his mistress, Nell Gwynne, was buried in the churchyard. Today the church has a good café and contains London's Brass Rubbing Centre.

Opposite South Africa House is the square's other column – a lamp standard that is a police station in disguise. Charles I cuts a fine figure on a horse in the fine equestrian statue by Hubert le Sueur that faces down Whitehall. Cast in 1633, the Civil War and loss of the monarchy intervened before it could be erected, and it was sold for scrap to a Mr Rivett, a brazier. Once Charles II was back on the throne, the statue was miraculously resurrected and set on the plinth, possibly designed by Sir Christopher Wren.

The Road to Power

Whitehall, the street leading from Trafalgar Square, once connected the City of London with the great Abbey of Westminster. It cuts through the site of a royal palace that was the seat of power. Now it is lined with public buildings, and finishes at the Palace of Westminster, a people's palace and the seat of democratic government. On the right is the **Horse Guards**, where the Household Cavalry, the Sovereign's bodyguard on state occasions, mount a picturesque daily ceremony – Changing the Guard (Mon–Sat at 11am, Sun 10am). Cameras click, horses nod, commands are shouted, and the troop returns to their Knightsbridge Barracks.

The **Banqueting House** (Mon–Sat 10am–5pm), facing the Horse Guards, is the only remaining building of Whitehall Palace. Following a fire which destroyed the original Tudor buildings, Inigo Jones was asked by James I to draw up plans for a new palace, but only the Banqueting House was built. Finished in 1622, it was probably London's first in Portland stone, and first in the style of Palladio. It must have looked astonishingly avant-garde rising from the huddle of timber-and-brick buildings. Inside, the Rubens ceiling provides a robust contrast to the architecture.

Cross back over to the Horse Guards and walk through the arch to **Horse Guards Parade**, where Trooping the Colour is performed on the Queen's official birthday. The best view is looking back across the parade ground at the Whitehall buildings.

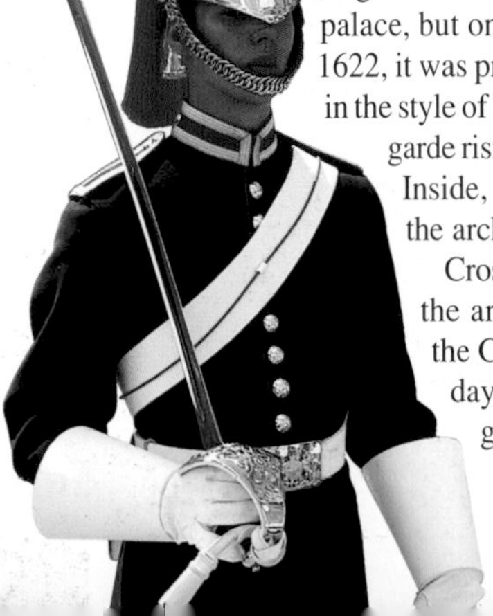

Above: Britain is governed from Whitehall
Left: a sentry stands guard

To the north lies the Admiralty, but return to Whitehall and head south to **Downing Street**, 'home' to the Prime Minister of the day since 1732. For security reasons, iron gates have sealed off the street from the general public since 1990. In the middle of Whitehall, opposite the next building down – the monumental Foreign Office – stands the Cenotaph. This was built by Edwin Lutyens to remember those who died in World War I. Now turn right down King Charles Street to reach the **Cabinet War Rooms** (daily 9.30am–6pm), the underground labyrinth from which Winston Churchill masterminded the strategy that finally released Londoners from the tyranny of the Luftwaffe in World War II.

Park Fashions

Ahead is the inviting peace of **St James's Park**. Henry VIII drained a swamp for it. Charles II had it decked out in the French taste with a straight canal, and let in the public to admire it. George IV's architect, John Nash, put a bend in the lake and gave it an island and a bridge with the best views in London. His landscaping is full of delightful incidents, disguising the fact that it is all on a very small scale, and visitors are entertained by a large variety of waterfowl. It's a favourite lunchtime spot for civil servants from the nearby government offices. There is a simple café near the northern end of the park, and lunch alternatives in Storey's Gate and on Victoria Street at that palace amongst pubs, the **Albert**.

Beyond the Mall, the wide processional way to Buckingham Palace, is Nash's **Carlton House Terrace**. The **Duke of York's Column**, on the site of Prince Regent's Mansion, was paid for by stopping a day's pay from all ranks of the army. Tucked under the terrace is the **Institute of Contemporary Arts** (daily noon–10.30pm or 1am, galleries till 7pm; inexpensive day membership required), with a gallery, cinema, café, bar and bookshop.

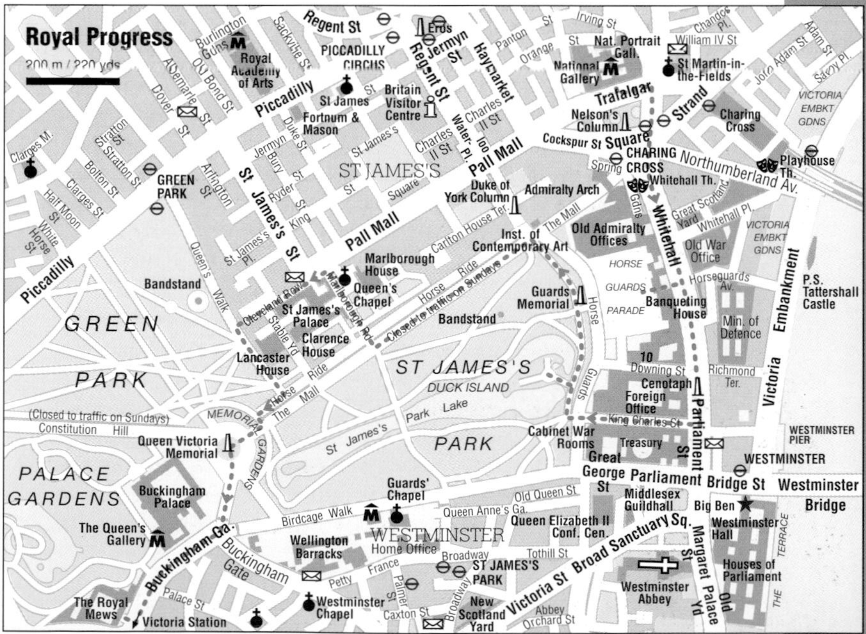

Next on the right down the Mall are the garden walls of **Marlborough House**, built by Wren. It was the home of Queen Mary, grandmother of the present Queen. In Marlborough Gate is the **Queen's Chapel**, designed by Inigo Jones, and built before the road existed. The interior can be viewed by worshippers on Sunday mornings, Easter to July.

St James's Palace, the 16th-century castellated brick building across the street, is where many royals were born (it is closed to the public). Proceed left past the guarded gatehouse, down Cleveland Row then through a passage into **Green Park**, laid out by Henry VIII. Take Queen's Walk, named after George II's queen, south past the grand neoclassical **Lancaster House**. This former museum building has been extravagantly refurbished for civic entertaining.

Evolution of a Palace

Buckingham Palace began life relatively humbly, in 1715, as the Duke of Buckingham's country house. What you see is architect Sir Aston Webb's façade of 1913; on the other side, facing the park, is John Nash's 1830s transformation for George IV. Strapped for cash to finish the job, Nash was replaced by the architect Edward Blore, whose work was largely wallpapered over by Webb. A limited number of the palace's state rooms (entrance in Buckingham Palace Road) are open to the public between August and October (daily 9.30am–4.30pm) when the Queen is always at Balmoral Castle in Scotland. The experience is expensive and somewhat disappointing, but outside the **Changing of the Guard** (11.30am daily, spring to autumn; every alternate day in winter), with the Queen in residence and the royal standard flying, is an impressive and colourful ceremony that has the edge on the Horse Guards. It is accompanied by music from the Guards' band.

The dull mix of Buckingham Palace Road is redeemed by the imposing entrance to the **Royal Mews** (Mon–Thurs noon–4pm, except Aug and Sept 10.30am–4.30pm). Here are the Queen's horses and coaches, including the Coronation Coach that was built for George III in 1762. The **Queen's Gallery** is closed until 2002 while extensive renovations are carried out. From here Victoria Station is just around the corner.

Above: Changing of the Guard at Buckingham Palace

3. West End *(see map, page 31)*

A tour of London's main shopping district from the once-fashionable Carnaby Street to the up-market tailors, wine merchants and antique dealers of St James's and Burlington Arcade, and the art galleries and jewellers of Mayfair – with a brief cultural diversion to the Royal Academy of Arts.

Start at Oxford Circus Station, Bakerloo, Central, Victoria lines

More than a geographical description of where the City leaves off, the name 'West End' confers on its inhabitants, workers and visitors alike, an accolade of breeding, affluence and fashion. That it most nearly identifies with the boundaries of Mayfair is no accident, nor that the Duke of Westminster's Grosvenor Estate covers most of that, and that Grosvenor is one of our richest men. The aristocrats have left their grand houses, and in their place are high-class hotels and restaurants, along with embassies and private clubs. Above all, there are shops, popular in Oxford Street, moving up-market through Regent Street to the refinement of Piccadilly and Bond Street. Shops, then, are the main attraction, but art galleries flourish too in the rich soil of the West End.

The first turning down Regent Street, Little Argyll Street, leads to the **London Palladium**, the Music Hall that followed a circus, where anything could happen on stage from *The Pirates of Penzance* to the Ram Jam Band, and probably will. In Great Marlborough Street you may be forgiven for thinking Mr Liberty a little backward-looking, but building his store **Liberty** in 'Tudor' style in 1924 showed him to be an astute businessman. The timbers are genuine enough; they came from England's wooden battleships. On the bridge that connects with the Regent Street building, St George rings bells and never quite succeeds in catching an elusive dragon every 15 minutes.

Liberty turns the corner into **Carnaby Street**. In the 1960s London swung highest here, and the street's name soon entered the Oxford English Dictionary to mean 'fashionable clothing for young people'. It still has its attractions but, despite recent refurbishment, it is a little threadbare, as Shakespeare might have said, 'by Time's fell hand defaced'. He looks down on the crowds from a niche on the corner of the **Shakespeare's Head**, though the pub's connection is not with William, but with Thomas and John Shakespeare, who owned the inn in 1735. The pervading smell in the street is of leather, usually black and studded with shiny metal decoration. The noise is the amplified thud of rock music. Many of the shops now sell tourist tat – from reproduction Abbey Road street signs (where the Beatles had their studios) to Union Jack underpants.

Above: St George charges over the clock outside Liberty

Turn right into Beak Street and continue down Regent Street, an elegant, though constantly traffic-congested, boulevard laid out in the early 1800s, and drop into the **Café Royal**. The plush gilt interior still evokes something of the attraction it had for Oscar Wilde, Aubrey Beardsley, Augustus John and other literary and artistic people, but the price of a drink will no longer buy you an evening's entertainment. Just across Regent Street is **Veeraswamy's Restaurant** (entrance at Victory House, 99–101 Swallow Street) which recalls the days of the British Raj.

Family Favourites

The hectic traffic intersection that is **Piccadilly Circus** has become a British synonym for anywhere that is very busy. It looks at its best at night, thanks to its giant illuminated advertising hoardings. On the south side stands the mis-named winged Eros, the God of Love – it was in fact erected to represent the Angel of Christian Charity. Have lunch, or at least take a peek, in the **Criterion** behind, owned by superchef Marco Pierre White: its decadent Byzantine decor is as memorable as the surprisingly affordable food. With kids in tow, you may want to head for Madame Tussaud's **Rock Circus** (Mar–Aug, daily 10am–8 or 9pm, rest of the year till 5.30pm), with waxwork pop stars, or the **Trocadero**, a tacky shopping mall with a Planet Hollywood restaurant, cinema and Segaworld (Mon–Sat 11am–11pm, Sun noon–10.30pm), which is a cross between a giant amusement arcade and virtual reality theme park.

For contrasting refinement, cross the circus to Lower Regent Street, and taste the teas in the **Ceylon Tea Centre** in Jermyn Street on the left. The latter is shopping by appointment to clubland and St James's. Windows offer ties, shirts, and shoes, with great discretion plus **Paxton & Whitfield** at No 93 with a choice of the best cheeses. Across the road, **St James's Church** was Wren's new church to serve a growing suburb. Badly damaged in World War II and recreated, it has a reredos of carved fruit and flowers and a carved marble 'garden of Eden' font by Grinling Gibbons. (More Gibbons is found in the angels that trumpet above the magnificent organ from the chapel of Whitehall Palace.) There is a crafts market in the pretty courtyard to the rear of the church.

Top: rendezvous under Eros on Piccadilly Circus
Above right: rock legends reside at Madame Tussaud's Rock Circus

The **Red Lion** in Duke of York Street is deceptively spacious inside, due to the cut-glass mirrors that surround the walls and produce endless reflections of their beautiful decoration, all set in the mahogany frame of the bar furniture. Down the hill is **St James's Square**, laid out in 1660 and with 18th-century houses that have seen the birth of a king, George III, and been the residence of the dukes of Norfolk, the bishops of London, and at No 10, Chatham House, of three prime ministers. This backwater has been touched violently by modern events. General Dwight D. Eisenhower planned the invasion of Africa and France here at No 31, and during a demonstration outside the Libyan People's Bureau in 1984 policewoman Yvonne Fletcher was shot dead. She is remembered in a memorial by the gardens' railing.

Shopping Georgian-style

Walk clockwise round the square's equestrian William III statue to King Street. Opposite **Christie's**, the famous auction rooms, is the **Golden Lion**, a drinking house with the second oldest licence in the West End, and a tiny bar which confers a quick intimacy on its customers. Take Crown Passage down to Pall Mall, then turn right to St James's Street and the remarkable survival of clubland's Georgian shopping parade. If you are a privileged customer at **Berry Bros and Rudd**, the wine merchants, they will record your weight on their giant scales, just as they did that of the Prince Regent, who might well have patronised **Lock & Co**, next door but one. Established in 1759, London's 'top' hatter has an interesting display in its windows. Between the shops is the narrow passage leading to **Pickering Place**, a Georgian backwater that it is difficult to associate with gambling and bloodshed, but it is credited with having been the scene of London's last duel.

Clubs, carefully guarding their anonymity, line the street. **Boodles**, at No 28, is perhaps everything it should be, with an imposing Adam-style front,

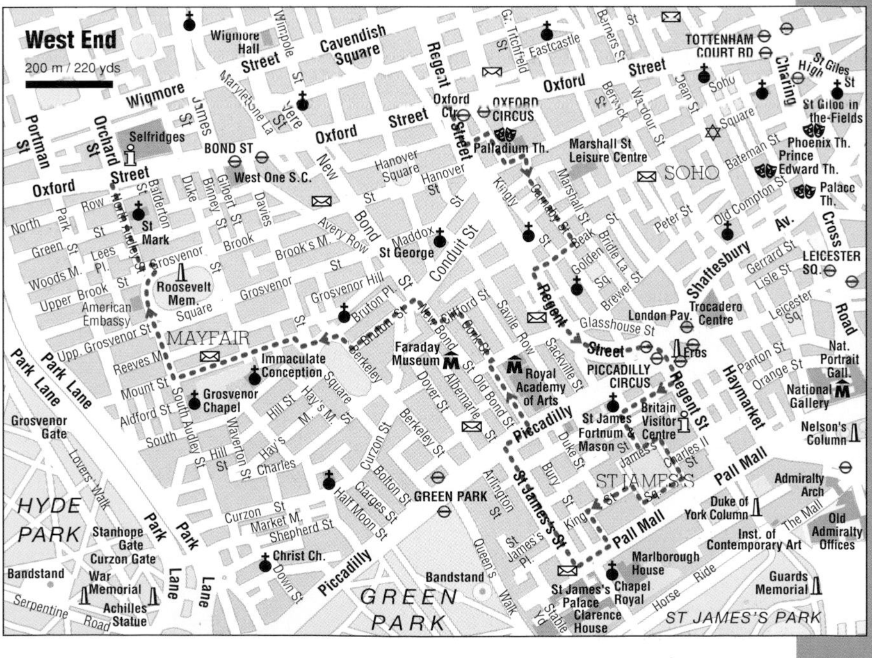

and a Venetian window which lights a very private world. Turn right onto Piccadilly and hope to catch the action on the hour of **Fortnum and Mason**'s clock. The shop's food hall is where the Queen buys her groceries; you can see the royal crest over the door. Enjoy the lively view from the restaurant before investigating Piccadilly's arcades.

What's Showing at the RA?

On the north side is Burlington House, the home of the **Royal Academy of Arts** (daily 10am–6pm, except Fri till 8.30pm),which in summer exhibits a selection of works for sale by living artists. At other times the Academy mounts high-profile exhibitions – often outstanding – to raise funds to help maintain its art school. The building itself entombs part of the Earl of Burlington's town house built in the 1660s, and occasional access can be had to a fine suite of rooms. The rest is ponderous Victorian.

The **Burlington Arcade**, next door, is frivolous by comparison, but that does not mean that you can whistle or even hurry through this promenade of tiny Regency shops. The top-hatted, tail-coated Beadles will apprehend you if you do. Jewellery is a speciality – look for the boutique selling Fabergé eggs.

Head across to **Cork Street**, which is almost wall-to-wall commercial galleries, all free. All shades of art appreciation are catered for, and feelings outraged at the Waddington Galleries can be soothed at Browse and Darby or the Redfern next door. Turn left into Clifford Street and from the right-hand side of New Bond Street look north to the **Time-Life Building**. Above the low-level link is a frieze by Henry Moore.

It is difficult to believe that **Bruton Street** was in such recent residential occupation that there could have been a royal birth here in the 1920s, but there is a plaque to prove it on the wall of Berkeley Square House, at the end on the left – 'Queen Elizabeth, born April 21, 1926'. **Berkeley Square**, covered in grand plane trees, has itself only lately succumbed to the gambling casinos and advertising agencies. The chinoiserie **Pump House** in the centre is still there, but the nightingale that – according to the famous song – once sang here, has long flown. On the west side a few good 18th-century houses linger on. **Mount Street**, which runs off the north-western corner of the square, is a confection in pink terracotta iced with the **Connaught**, the hotel with the enviable reputation, Scott's seafood restaurant, and the Audley, the pub with the 'English Dining Room'.

Under the watchful eye of the eagle above the United States Embassy (heavily guarded, as you will soon discover if you loiter, but notice the pugilistic statue of Dwight Eisenhower), South Audley Street engages Grosvenor Square, and leaves as North Audley Street for Oxford Street. Head this way if you feel the urge for more shopping. **Selfridges** anybody?

Left: another string to her bow
Above Right: the Tower of London

4. Tower and City *(see map, below)*

Contrasting faces of the City of London: ancient archaeological remains; the modern Design Museum; the Crown Jewels; restored Docklands, and restaurants where gents dine on oysters and champagne.

Do the walk on a weekday (the City is dormant at weekends); start at Tower Hill Station (District and Circle Tube lines)

From the beginning, the Tower and the City were the power and the glory of England's capital by the Thames, exercising military and monetary control often with a crushing disregard for human life. For nearly 400 years traitors imprisoned in the Tower were brought to Tower Hill above the river for public execution, the exact spot recorded by a stone pavement in **Trinity Square Gardens**. Heads rolled but others were saved. Nearby, in the elegant, 18th-century Trinity House, the Trinity Brethren built lighthouses and provided pilots for greater safety at sea. Beside them on the hill are several stretches of the City's **Roman wall**.

Turn your back on the monstrous former headquarters of the Port of London Authority topped by the statue of Neptune, and look riverwards to the **Tower of London** (Mar–Oct: Mon–Sat 9am–6pm, Sun 10am–6pm, last guided tour 3.30pm; Nov–Feb: closes at 5pm, last guided tour 2.30pm), which surely inspires every child's toy fort. William the Conqueror's White Tower, Eng-

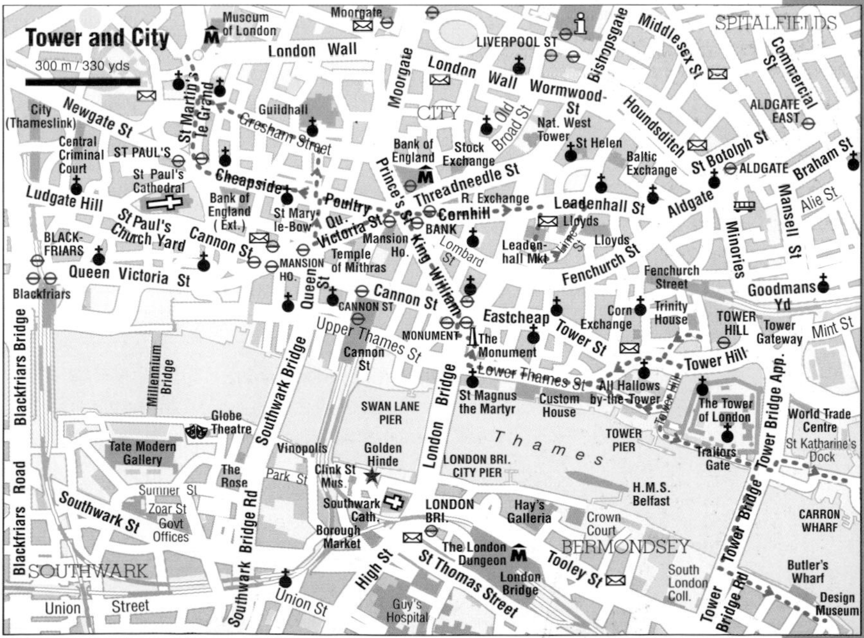

land's only complete Norman keep, dominates the surrounding walls and bastions, its corner turrets renewed, like capped teeth, in the 14th century. Inside is the **Chapel of St John**, looking as if it had been hollowed from solid rock, immensely impressive in its strength and simplicity. As an antidote take in the **Crown Jewels** and see what Charles II wore on formal occasions, or hear from a picturesquely garbed Beefeater just why ravens are on the payroll (legend says that if they ever leave, the Tower will crumble). The wharf along the river gives a different view of **Traitors' Gate** from that enjoyed by the wretches landed here by boat.

Tower Bridge (Apr–Oct: daily 10am–6.30pm; Nov–March: daily 9.30am–6pm, last admission 4.45pm) is the perfect accompaniment to the Tower; it conceals the engineering expertise of the Victorians (it was built in 1894) in raising by steam the great bascules of the road bridge – which is still done some 500 times a year. The high-level walkway gives a great view of *HMS Belfast*. If you are feeling energetic, then cross the bridge briefly to the regenerated Butler's Wharf, with its excellent restaurants and the Conran Foundation **Design Museum** (daily 11.30am–6pm). Meet old and familiar friends here – everyday things like a bicycle or a chair – and learn why they look like they do, or did. A regular ferry service (11am–5pm) connects the wharf to the other nearby attractions on the river.

Dockland Heritage

The Tower Thistle Hotel introduces **St Katharine's Dock**, which has taken on a new life as London's marina. Telford's fine warehouses, once piled with ivory tusks, are the backdrop for Thames barges and restored old clippers, and an 18th-century warship *The Grand Turk*. You can enjoy a drink at one of the several waterside cafés or in the nautically ambient **Dickens Inn**.

The drab Lower Thames Street runs from the Tower, past the Custom House (cross to the left side) to **St Magnus the Martyr**. Wren's richly furnished in-

Above: Tower Bridge
Right: the griffin is the City's symbol

terior survives – pulpit and tester, gallery, organ of 1712, and altar paintings of high quality. Up Fish Street Hill stands the **Monument** (Mon–Fri 10am–5.40pm, weekends 2–5.40pm), erected in 1671–7 by Wren to commemorate the Great Fire. In the relief on the pedestal Charles II cheers on the rebuilding of the devastated City, dressed improbably as a Roman. Catholics will be glad to learn that they are no longer blamed for the catastrophe, the original inscription having been changed. Not for the faint-hearted is the 202ft (61.5m) climb up the spiral stair for spectacular views.

Houses of Money and God

From here take King William Street, a spoke in the wheel that revolves around the hub of financial London, to **Royal Exchange**, the Lord Mayor's residence, the **Mansion House**, and the **Bank of England**. The bank has an excellent museum on Bartholomew Lane (Mon–Fri 10am–5pm), with specimens of centuries-old banknotes. In such company a lesser building than the parish church of **St Mary Woolnoth** at the corner of Lombard Street would be outfaced, but Hawksmoor's twin towers more than hold their own, even though Tube station entrances burrow beneath. The name Woolnoth, so it is said inside, was given to illegitimate children when they were baptised.

Tucked behind the columned and pedimented front of the Mansion House is another Wren creation, **St Stephen Walbrook church**, on Walbrook, which is poised above a hidden stream. Walk up the steps and you are climbing Walbrook's bank. With St Stephen, Wren was obviously feeling his way towards St Paul's dome and lantern over a central space. Now the eye goes to Henry Moore's massive altar table, pagan almost in its primitive simplicity. In complete contrast a glorious organ looks down on the circling, contemporary seats.

Turn left into Queen Victoria Street for Temple Court, and in its forecourt the remains of the excavated **Temple of Mithras**, brought from the site of Bucklersbury House nearby, and strangely elevated and isolated among forbidding office blocks. **Sweetings**, the fish restaurant on the corner of Queen Street, looks older and has all the earmarks of an authentic City institution – marble slabs, crisp white linen, and City men and women on stools and in a hurry downing their oysters. Cross, right, to Bow Lane and so to Cheapside's **St Mary-le-Bow**. Wren's magnificent tower and steeple escaped the fires of the Blitz that destroyed the bells. Gutted and restored, the body of the church has little charm and, mystifyingly, two pulpits.

Turn right down Cheapside and left into King Street. Beyond its yard is the **Guildhall** (daily 10am–5pm, closed Sun in winter). There is little medieval about it now, except for its outline, but fires, bombing and modern additions fail to diminish its status as one of London's most important civic buildings. Guests at the frequent banquets share the Great Hall with Nelson and Welling-

Right: the church of St Stephen Walbrook

ton, a leaden Churchill and, above the gallery, the gilded figures of Gog and Magog, the City's giants. Sir Nicholas Throckmorton was not so lucky. An inscription records that at his trial in the hall for high treason, the jury's verdict of not guilty was deemed unsatisfactory, and they were sent to prison themselves until they came up with a more acceptable result.

At the rear of Guildhall to the left you will find the **Guildhall Library** (Mon–Sat 9.30am–5pm), where one of the City guilds, the Worshipful Company of Clockmakers, puts on a permanent exhibition of their considerable contribution to horology (not open Sat). More fascinating still is the **Museum of London** (Tues–Sat 10am–5.50pm, Sun noon–5.50pm, closed Mon), which reached by continuing up Gresham Street and turning right up to the busy roundabout where the museum sits. Inside you will find all the best archaeological finds discovered in the City over the past four decades, plus the Lord Mayor's glittering coach.

Traditional Spirit of the City

From the museum head south along St Martin's Le Grand, turn left along Cheapside and Poultry and then cross the Bank intersection into Cornhill. If the spirit of the old City exists anywhere it is here in the maze of little courts and alleys between Cornhill and Lombard Street. **Ball Court** on the right (follow a sign to Simpson's) plunges you into the world of Thackeray and Dickens, with surprises at every turn. Here is **Simpson's** (open since 1759) with inviting offerings of steak and kidney pie and favourite steamed puddings in dignified surroundings. A taste of the 18th century? Hard by at the **George and Vulture** Mr Pickwick is in the chair of the Pickwick Club, and in St Michael's Alley, history tells us that **Pasqua Rosée** served London's first cup of coffee

in 1652. Above a tiny space where parishioners were buried, Hawksmoor's tower of **St Michael Cornhill** thrusts upwards to the light. Below, the **Jamaica Wine House** revels in the dark.

Just short of Gracechurch Street is a view of Wren's **St Peter upon Cornhill**, slotted between shops and offices, and smug in its claim to have beaten Canterbury as the earliest consecrated ground in England. Thackeray, in the editorial chair of the *Cornhill Magazine*, could see the church from his window. Pause at the street corner and look left: at the foot of the shining black **NatWest Tower** is the white, wedding-cake extravagance of the former National Provincial Bank, dock leaf to NatWest's nettle.

Cross to Leadenhall Street, and, first right on Whittington Avenue is **Leadenhall Market**, a fine covered arcade. It was a meat market in the 14th century, and you can still buy meat here, though there's other produce too, and attractive cafés and pubs. Christmases past, when it was festooned with turkeys to the heights of its Victorian glass-and-iron roof, are remembered by older Londoners. The site of the market was the centre of Roman London, and below it was a basilica nearly as long as St Paul's Cathedral.

Lime Street, where the shipping lines come ashore, curves round the market to Richard Rogers's **Lloyd's Building**, where insurance underwriting, once conducted under Adam ceilings in a 1920s building, now operates from a glass-and-satin-steel complex with its guts revealed for all to see from the outside. Watching the crawler lifts slide up and down the outside is a local pastime. The No 25 bus stop (for Oxford Street) is on Leadenhall Street.

5. South Bank *(see map, pages 38–9)*

A riverside walk that takes in exciting new attractions along a stretch of the Thames billed as the Millennium Mile, also passing some of the city's great artistic institutions and the London that Shakespeare knew. This long walk offers constant views over the Thames, and is enjoyable even if you don't visit many of the sights.

Start at Westminster Station (District, Jubilee and Circle Tube lines)

Cross Westminster Bridge and head for the monumental 'Edwardian Renaissance' County Hall building on your left. Home of the Greater London Council until it was disbanded in 1986, it now contains two hotels and several attractions. The newest is the **FA Premier League Hall of Fame** (Mon–Fri 10.30am–6.30pm, weekends from 10am), where tableaux tell the story of football, and wide-eyed fans ogle at waxworks of their favourite stars. Just around the corner on The Queen's Walk, the **London Aquarium** (daily 10am–6pm) houses a remarkable collection of aquatic species from all over the world in cleverly simulated habitats.

Above left: Sweetings fish restaurant
Left: Leadenhall Market. **Right:** the London Eye

You'll probably have already spotted the biggest new landmark raised in central London in years – the towering **London Eye** (Apr–Oct: daily 9am–10pm; rest of the year: daily 10am–6pm). The white Ferris wheel, erected at the end of 1999, cost £20 million to install, and is the largest of its kind in the world. It has an official lifespan of only five years, but may prove popular enough to become a permanent attraction. On a clear day, from the top of the 30-minute ride you can in theory see seven counties and Windsor Castle.

Arts Set in Concrete

Continue along the riverside walk to the **South Bank Centre**, a group of brutalist, concrete buildings that together amount to London's most important arts complex. The **Royal Festival Hall** (foyer exhibitions and informal musical performances daily 10am–10.30pm) is the sole survivor of the Festival of Britain of 1951. Inside are great spaces for grand occasions, and changing exhibitions that fill the main and upper foyers and the riverside terrace. There is lunchtime music (Wed–Sun) and a choice of buffets and bars. Next door are the **Queen Elizabeth Hall** and the **Purcell Room**, both venues for classical concerts, and the **Hayward Gallery** (Thurs–Mon 10am–6pm, Tues and Wed till 8pm), London's most important venue for big contemporary art exhibitions.

Outside by the river there is more than a hint of Paris in the bookstalls under Waterloo Bridge. Behind them stands a temple to cinema, the **National Film Theatre**, which screens high-brow movies and puts on talks and lectures. The Museum of the Moving Image, until recently housed in the same build-

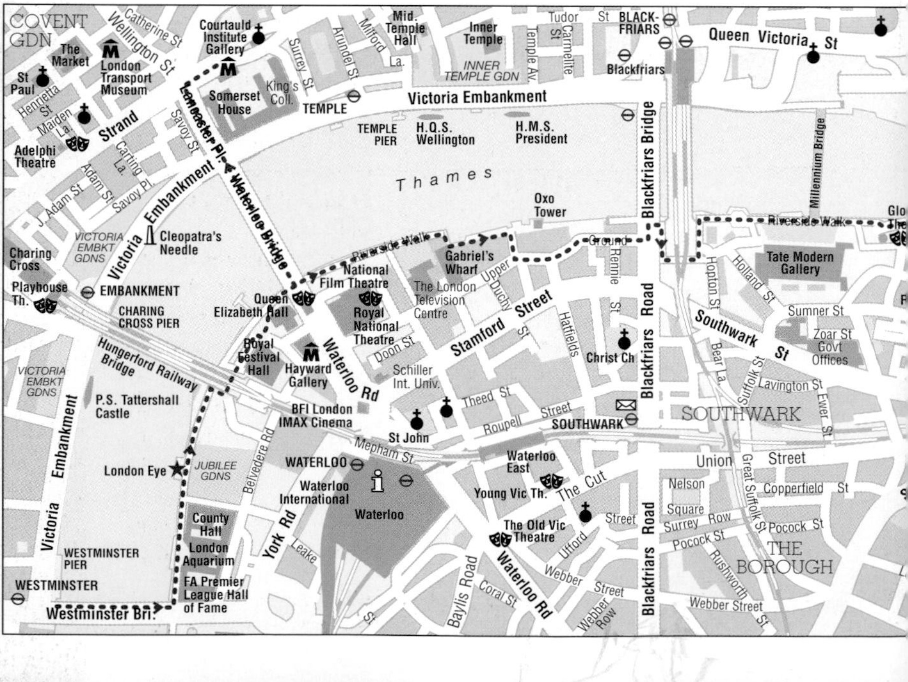

ing, is currently closed for rebuilding. However, film buffs may want to make their way to the new **BFI London IMAX Cinema**, just behind Waterloo Bridge, on a spot once known as 'Cardboard City' where many of London's homeless lived. The eye-catching, glass-encased circular building in the middle of a roundabout has Britain's largest cinema screen – 65ft (20 metres) high and 85ft (26 metres) wide), on which films suited to the IMAX format on such topics as space and the ocean are shown daily from 11am–10pm.

Before heading east along the river to the last of the South Bank's concrete monsters, the Royal National Theatre, you might want to detour over Waterloo Bridge to the **Courtauld Institute** (Mon–Sat 10am–6pm, Sun noon–6pm) in Somerset House. Its outstanding collection includes some of the world's best-known Impressionist and Post-Impressionist paintings.

Back on the South Bank past the **Royal National Theatre**, with its three excellent theatres and more bars and cafés, you pass **Gabriel's Wharf**, a pleasant clutch of cafés and crafts shops on a refreshing human scale after what's gone before. A little further along is the **OXO Tower**, where a giant advertisement for the eponymous stock cubes was once sited. The eighth floor has been turned into a smart restaurant and brasserie, but even if you don't want to eat, take the lift up to admire the view from the public gallery.

Go through the underpass under Blackfriars Bridge. Ahead lies the colossal brick edifice of what was the Bankside Power Station and is now the **Tate Gallery of Modern Art**, an offshoot of its parent across the river. It houses the Tate's international art collection. At its far end, notice the old building at

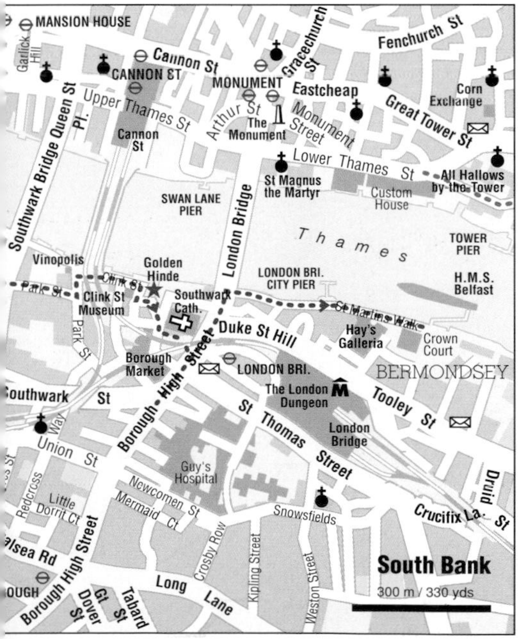

Left: crafts this way
Above: view from the Oxo Tower

the entrance to Cardinal Cap Alley: it is sometimes claimed that Sir Christopher Wren lived here while St Paul's was built. The **Millennium Bridge**, a pedestrian link between the new Tate Gallery and St Paul's which opened in 2000, is the first new bridge to span the Thames in central London for over a century.

Tudor Theatres

In Shakespeare's time, Londoners took a boat to the theatre. The City had banished acting – along with bear- and bull-baiting and brothels – to the south bank of the river. Bear Gardens led to the 'baiting ring', new in 1550. Sixty years later it was replaced by The Hope – one of four theatres that once stood here on Bankside – where Ben Jonson's *Bartholemew Fair* was produced. A replica of the open-air **Globe Theatre** opened in 1996 after years of fund-raising by the inspired American actor Sam Wanamaker, who sadly died before its completion. It even has a thatched roof – the first to be allowed in London since the Great Fire of 1666. As well as plays from May–Sept, there is an exhibition and you can take a guided tour of the theatre (May–Sept: daily 9am–noon; rest of the year: daily 10am–5pm).

The Globe's original site is round the corner on Park Street (just east of Southwark Bridge). On the way, take a look at the site of **The Rose** (daily 10am–5pm), the oldest Bankside theatre, built in 1587. Its remains, now flooded and encased in concrete to protect them, were discovered in 1989 when a building was demolished. Campaigners ensured that the new office block built over the site did not disturb them, though their accessibility is less than ideal. An exhibition tells the story.

At Bank End is the friendly **Anchor** pub, where little has changed in over 200 years. Across the street, in the labyrinth of brick-lined vaults under the railway viaduct, is **Vinopolis** (daily 10am–5.30pm), another imagi-

Top: the reconstructed Globe Theatre
Above: sign for the 17th-century George Inn

native, large-scale new attraction billed as the world's first wine theme park. It features two fun and educational galleries, wine tastings, a well-stocked wine shop, and a restaurant offering over 200 wines by the glass.

Down Clink Street once stood the Bishop of Westminster's 13th-century town residence, its surviving fragments now trapped in the fabric of Victorian warehouses. The bishop's prison, 'The Clink', gave its name to the street and became a slang term for prison. 'Material of an explicit nature' is shown in the **Clink Street Museum** (daily 10am–6pm). Time was when parishioners could land goods free of toll at St Mary Overy Dock around the corner, or have their wives put in the ducking stool. The **Golden Hinde** (daily 10am–dusk), an exact replica of Sir Francis Drake's diminutive ship, now fills the dock.

Round the corner **Southwark Cathedral** is a treasure house of church relics. John Harvard, a church warden's son christened here in 1607, was the benefactor of Harvard University, partly with money from the sale of the Queen's Head in Borough High Street, one of the many galleried inns that lined the approach to London Bridge. Of these, only the **George** (at No 77) still exists. The scrubbed wood, open hearth and galleried yard evoke the 1670s.

London Bridge Station is a short walk north, or, if you still have a spring in your step, you could return to the river and follow the waterside path again along the old **Hay's Wharf**. In the 19th century, tea clippers from India and China docked here. Now there are mainly office blocks, though **Hay's Galleria**, where the original wharf has been filled in and given a glass roof to form an atrium of cafés and shops, is pleasant. The World War II cruiser **HMS Belfast** (Mar–Oct: daily 10am–6pm; rest of the year till 5pm) is moored a little further along the riverfront.

6. War and Peace *(see map, page 42)*

Relive the Blitz at the Imperial War Museum, then visit the Houses of Parliament and Westminster Abbey. Watch Parliament in session, or go to see the best of Turner's paintings at the Tate Gallery.

Start at Lambeth North Station (Bakerloo Tube line)

This walk begins where the futility of war is recorded, in the old Bethlem Royal Hospital for the Insane. As a home for the **Imperial War Museum** (daily 10am–6pm), 'Bedlam', as the hospital was popularly called, was an inspired choice. Its special-effects 'The Blitz Experience' brings home what Londoners went through during World War II, but more powerful is the 'Trench Experience' which successfully conveys the horror of the trenches in World War I. What is not generally appreciated by the public is the importance of the museum's collection of work by official war artists. This includes a series of paintings of Clyde shipbuilding by Stanley Spencer, works by Paul Nash and Graham Sutherland, and moving images painted during World War I by Nevinson.

Right: lethal weapon, the Imperial War Museum

About a half mile down the rather bleak Lambeth Road are the Palace of the Archbishop of Canterbury and the deconsecrated parish church of St Mary's, born again as the **Museum of Garden History** (Mon–Fri, 10.30am–4pm, Sun 10.30am–5pm). With no parishioners it needed friends, and the gardeners of the Tradescant Trust not only rescued the church from decay but created a museum and a garden. The Tradescants, who lived locally, were gardeners to Lord Salisbury and Charles I. The replica 17th-century garden, reached through the church, is planted with flowers and shrubs they brought from abroad. John Tradescant died in 1638, and is buried here. Nearby lies Captain Bligh of the *Bounty*. He was also a plant hunter, and it was on an expedition to Tahiti to collect bread-fruit that the famous mutiny broke out.

A Palace, Pineapples and Parliament

Lambeth Palace, London home of the Archbishops of Canterbury for over 700 years, was on the river by the ferry steps until bridge and embankment put it across the road, but the group of buildings by St Mary's still makes an attractive composition. The twin-towered, red brick gatehouse known as **Morton's Tower** was built in 1495; behind it is a 17th-century hall. The palace has begun offering regular guided tours for the first time (Tues–Sat 10.30am–3.15pm; booking advisable on tel: 020-7898 1198). The pineapples topping the pillars at the bridge approach are a 'thank you' to John Tradescant, the man who first brought them to England. Across the road from the palace is a riverside promenade with a good view of Parliament; TV interviews with politicians are sometimes staged here.

Cross Lambeth Bridge towards the grand civil service and defence buildings and descend the steps on the right to the Victoria Tower Gardens. At the far end near the **Houses of Parliament** is a sombre group: the *Burghers of*

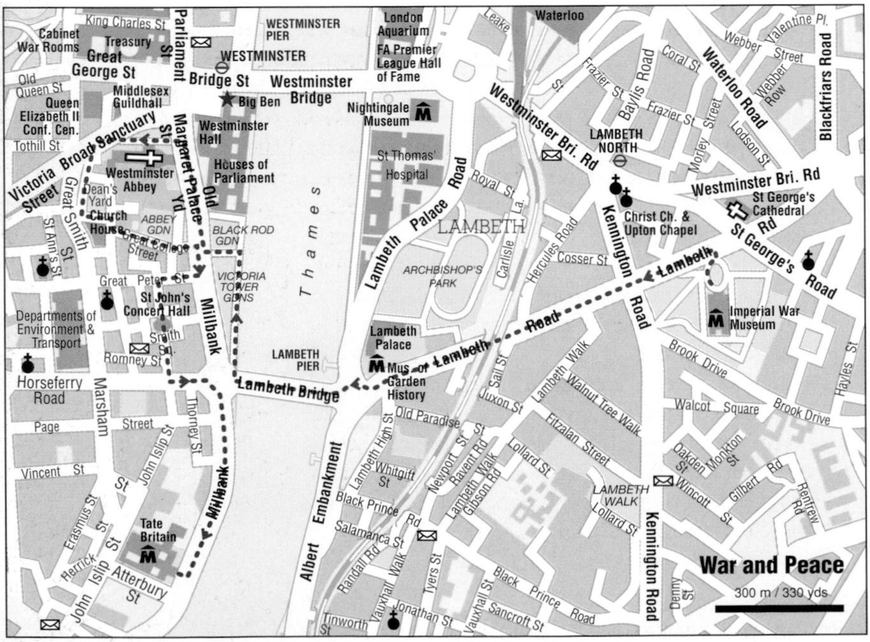

Calais, Rodin's expression in bronze of compassion for the fate of the hostages to Edward III. **Great College Street** opens opposite. Here, on the right, is the abbey's moat wall. Below ground ran one of Tyburn's streams, which isolated Thorney Island on which Westminster Abbey stood.

At the turn in the street is the entry to the very imposing and old **Dean's Yard**, and on the right the restored monastic buildings of **Westminster School**, which had its origins in the abbey itself and provides the singers for the Abbey choir. Leave Dean's Yard through the arch of the Victorian office block on the far side, and the west front entrance to **Westminster Abbey** (Mon–Fri 9.30am–4.45pm, Sat 9.30am–2.45pm; entry fee) is on your right. What is so remarkable about this cathedral-like building is that it is not in ruins, which it probably would be had it not been the crowning and burial place of kings and queens, the seat of government even. This special dispensation did not protect it from restorers, however, and, looking at the west towers, its most prominent aspect, there is little hint of the Norman French abbey behind. What we see is English, and 18th-century English at that. Wren proposed and Hawksmoor disposed.

Inside the Abbey

The main entrance is through the north porch. Follow the crowds round to the **Lady Chapel**, also known as Henry VII's Chapel. Not completed until 1519, it is the most architecturally exciting part of the abbey with its spectacular fan-vaulted roof and huge windows made possible by the flying buttresses. Henry was said to be remembered long after the 10,000 masses for his soul had been said. Over the stalls hang the banners and crests of the Knights of the Bath. Facing the entrance to the chapel is the graffitied Coronation Chair, used at every monarch's coronation since the early 1300s. It was designed to hold the Stone of Scone, stolen from the Scots in 1296 and returned to them exactly 700 years later; the stone is now kept in Edinburgh Castle.

Poet's Corner is the abbey's biggest draw. It began with Chaucer, buried here in 1400, but got out of hand in the 18th century, when it started to resemble a sculpture room at the Victoria and Albert Museum. The tombs and monuments amount to a roll-call of the great and the sometimes good of English arts (not just poetry).

The tour now leaves the body of the church for the

Above: Westminster Abbey
Right: fan vaulting in the Lady Chapel inside the abbey

cloisters, where the Benedictine monks would have worked on manuscripts, and were laid to rest. Off the cloisters lies the **Chapter House** (Apr–Oct: daily 10am–5.30pm; rest of the year till 4pm), where the Great Council met in 1257. From the time of Edward I to Henry VIII, it was used as Parliament House for the Commons, and to this day the Dean and Chapter have no authority here. Admission to the Chapter House also covers the **Abbey Museum** (daily 10.30am–4pm) in the Norman undercroft, a mini-Tussaud's of life-like effigies (including Henry VII, Elizabeth I, Charles II and Nelson) made for funeral processions. Beyond is the entrance to the **College Garden** (Apr–Sept: Tues and Thurs 10am–6pm; rest of the year till 4pm), used by the monks for growing herbs. There is evidence that it was laid out on a bed of oyster shells for drainage.

You leave the abbey via the nave, where Henry Yevele's work in the 14th century blends into Henry de Reyn's of a century earlier. Its astounding proportions lift the eyes to the roof, the highest in England.

Power Moves to Gothic

Outside, bear right round the abbey to get to **St Margaret Westminster**, the parliamentary place of worship. Cross the street to the Houses of Parliament. One building stands out against the Victorian Gothic, the medieval **Westminster Hall**, sole survivor of the Palace of Westminster after the fire of 1834 and described as 'the finest timber-roofed building in Europe'. For hundreds of years it served as the law courts, where death was dispensed to kings, bishops, earls and conspirators, including Guy Fawkes. We could have had an Elizabethan-style Parliament, but the taste for Gothic prevailed and by 1860 the two Houses, designed by Barry with Pugin as his assistant, were completed. Barry was knighted; Pugin went insane. The visitors' galleries of the **House of Commons** and **House of Lords** allow viewing when they are in session (from 2.30pm most weekdays); join the queues at St Stephen's Entrance.

In Millbank turn right into Great Peter Street and left into **Lord North Street**, where bells ring in the Georgian houses to summon MPs to vote on divisions in the House. At the end is the silhouette of **St John Smith Square**. Condemned as 'Queen Anne's Footstool', Thomas Archer's idiosyncratic church was burned out during the last war and was turned into a concert hall.

Regain Millbank via Horseferry Road and continue to the **Tate Gallery** (daily 10am–5.50pm). When the Tate Gallery of Modern Art opens across the river (*see pages 39–40*) this gallery will hand over its collection of international 20th-century art to concentrate on its role as a repository of British art from the 15th century onwards (including the world's biggest Turner collection in the **Clore Gallery**) and showcase for contemporary British artists. The Victoria Line's Pimlico station is across Vauxhall Bridge Road.

Above: inside tthe Tate Gallery
Above right: Chelsea Royal Hospital

7. CHELSEA *(see map, below)*

A Wednesday or Sunday afternoon visit to London's oldest garden and the homes of many famous writers, with a glimpse of sunset on the Thames.

Start at Sloane Square (Circle and District Tube lines or bus from Piccadilly)

There is more to Chelsea than just the famous King's Road. A few steps away from the boutiques, antique arcades and burger bars is the riverside village that Whistler loved to paint. Not that King's Road doesn't have a good start. See how wonderfully the designers of **Peter Jones**, the department store, managed the transition from square to street in a deliciously sensuous curve.

On the other side of Sloane Square is the **Royal Court**, a theatre with a talent for iconoclastic experiment. Lower Sloane Street leads off the south side to Royal Hospital Road and, just past the Old Burial Ground, the main gate of Chelsea's **Royal Hospital** (Mon–Sat 10am–noon and 2–4pm, Sun 2–4pm). Charles II took a leaf out of Louis XIV's book in providing a home for his old and disabled soldiers, and modelled it on the Hotel des Invalides in Paris. Sir Christopher Wren was appointed architect, and what could have been a forbidding institution was handled with great sympathy. The **Chapel**, consecrated in 1691 and featuring a splendid *Resurrection* painted by Sebastiano Ricci, and the **Great Hall**, where the Chelsea pensioners, retired war

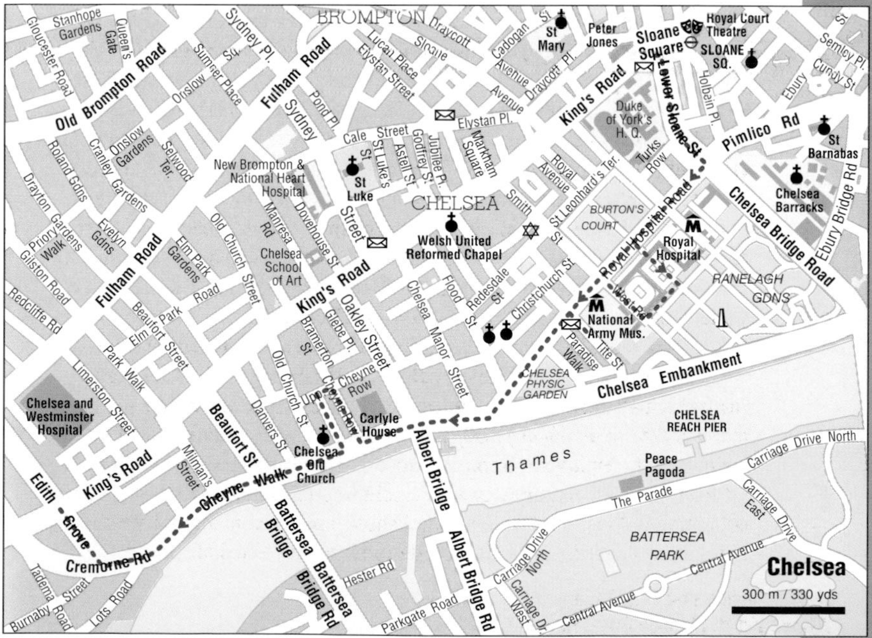

veterans who wear distinctive red uniforms, eat their meals under the gaze of Verrio's *Charles II on Horseback*, are most rewarding. The **museum** has several surprising exhibits, such as tortoiseshell ear trumpets. At the eastern end of the grounds is a garden on the site of one of London's famous 18th-century pleasure grounds: Ranelagh.

Leave the path through the hospital at the western end in Infirmary Road, and regain Royal Hospital Road past the stables. Here turn left into Tite Street, where No 34 was Oscar Wilde's 'House Beautiful', from which he edited *Woman's World*.

The entrance to **Chelsea Physic Garden** (Apr–Oct: Wed noon–5pm, Sun 2–6pm) is in Swan Walk. Founded by the Society of Apothecaries in 1673, it is second only to Oxford as the oldest botanic garden in the country, with thousands of rare and unusual plants including the largest olive tree outdoors in Britain and tea.

Homes of the Rich and Famous

Head on down to Chelsea Embankment. **Cheyne Walk** crosses Oakley Street and continues past the houses of the rich and influential, where even the street parking is for 'Diplomats' Cars Only'. Gardens and a road now separate it from the river, which was once lined with the cottages and wharves of Chelsea village. Turn right into Cheyne Row, which has a good pub in the King's Head and Eight Bells, and find that time stands still in **Carlyle House** (Apr–Oct: Wed–Sun and Bank Holidays 11am–5pm). The Scottish historian, Thomas Carlyle, brought his wife Jane here in 1834, to live in a house built in the early 1700s. They left it wholly Victorian, papering over the panelling, and it remains with its books, furniture and pictures just as they left them. What the 'Sage of Chelsea' did not find was peace and quiet. His sound-proof attic study, built on the roof, failed to keep out the noise of cocks crowing, street musicians and horses' hooves. How would he have reacted to living under today's flightpath?

At the end of Cheyne Row turn left into Upper Cheyne Row and **Lawrence Street**, home of the Chelsea porcelain works from 1745–84. Dr Johnson fancied his hand at the wheel, but his pots never survived the firing. Halfway down Lawrence Street is a fascinating byway, **Justice Walk**, but continue on to Cheyne Walk and to confrontation with a lumpen, gilded Sir Thomas More, Chelsea's most important resident. Henry VIII's Chancellor went to the Tower, and was beheaded in 1535, having prepared his resting place in **Chelsea Old Church**. The church was nearly destroyed by a

Above: beer stop at The Man in the Moon, King's Road
Right: one of the Edwardian food halls at Harrods

land mine in 1941 but, like the Portland vase, was lovingly reassembled from the shattered fragments and looks, you could say, as good as old. Amongst many distinguished monuments to distinguished people are two carved capitals by Holbein.

Further west, across Church Street on Danvers Street, is **Crosby Hall**, Chelsea's oldest house, yet only here since 1910. It was originally in Bishopsgate, the great hall of a wool merchant's mansion built between 1466 and 1475, though sadly it is no longer open to the public. The view upriver from the west end of Cheyne Walk can, given a sunset, still be a romantic one, and it may have contributed to the decisions of so many of the famous in art and literature to live here – Whistler and Brunel in Lindsey House, Hilaire Belloc, Walter Greaves, Wilson Steer and Turner. Suddenly the road turns away from the river at **Cremorne**, a sad scrap of garden where Victorians danced the night away beneath the coloured lanterns. Edith Grove on the right will take you back to the King's Road. A long, but fun walk past its shops will take you back to Sloane Square, or you can catch a bus.

8. BELGRAVIA, KNIGHTSBRIDGE AND SOUTH KENSINGTON *(see map, page 48)*

Start at lunchtime with a choice of interesting pubs serving food in upmarket Belgravia, then on to Harrods and a choice of three splendid museums: the V&A, the Natural History Museum and the Science Museum.

Start at Hyde Park Corner (Piccadilly Tube line or bus from Piccadilly)

A roundabout too big, yet not big enough for so much traffic makes **Hyde Park Corner** a dangerous place to stand and stare. So slip away down Knightsbridge, and take the unpromising alley on the left into **Old Barrack Yard**. The Duke of Wellington paraded his men here before Waterloo, and stabled his horse through the archway on the right in the mews. His mounting block can still be seen outside **The Grenadier** public house.

Turn left into Wilton Row and right into Wilton Crescent to Wilton Place. Opposite St Paul's is the narrow entrance to Kinnerton Street, once the village street for coachmen and grooms, butlers and manservants. Thinly disguised, the coach houses and haylofts are there still, and so are the pubs. The tiny **Nag's Head** is known as 'the £11 pub', the sum it was bought for in 1923. Motcomb Street vies with Bond Street as the artists' shop window. Most of the galleries welcome casual visitors, although you may need to ring the doorbell before being admitted. An inviting arcade leads to West Halkin Street. Cross left and turn the corner to the arched entrance of Belgrave Mews West, the service road to Belgrave Square's mansions. **The Star** is just about everything a public house should be, quiet and welcoming.

Back under the mews arch, turn right into **Belgrave Square**, so large the other side is out of sight. The square is the location of many foreign embassies. The sheer scale of its facades makes it a difficult place to come to terms with, and it is a relief to leave its southwest corner for Pont Street. Continue through Cadogan Square, and think of Oscar Wilde sitting in Room 53 of the **Cadogan Hotel**, getting quietly drunk while waiting to be arrested.

Grocer's Shop Made Good

Pont Street finishes beyond Sloane Street and continues into **Beauchamp Place**, where the mix of shops, restaurants and boutiques makes a colourful street scene. A few hundred yards/metres right in the Brompton Road was a small grocer's shop lit, in 1848, by paraffin lamps. Today, **Harrods** is the largest store in Europe. The **Food Hall** defies superlatives, the art deco gentlemen's hairdresser is a delight, and so, I am told, is the ladies' lavatory.

To the left on the other side of Brompton Road is the **Victoria and Albert Museum** (Tues–Sun 10am–5.45pm, Mon noon–5.45pm), built after the Great Exhibition of 1851 was held in Hyde Park. (The Victorians were rude about

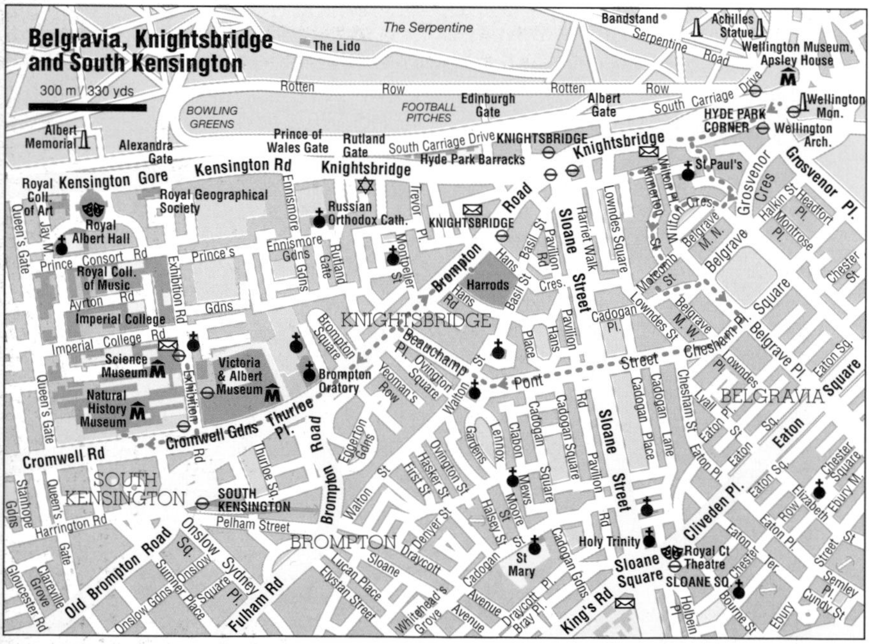

it, but the iron-and-glass construction survived to roof the East End's Museum of Childhood.) The V&A, one of a clutch of museums centred on Exhibition Road, was completed in 1909, and contains a superlative collection of decorative arts too large to detail and displayed over 7 miles (11km) of galleries. Just across Exhibition Road is the **Natural History Museum** (Mon–Sat 10am–5.50pm, Sun 11am–5.50pm). In a curious way the Romanesque extravagance of the Victorian building suits the stuffed elephants and dinosaur skeletons displayed inside. The old Geological Museum has been turned into the Natural History Museum's excellent Earth Galleries, which offer an engaging escalator ride through a giant revolving globe.

Also in Exhibition Road is the **Science Museum** (daily 10am–6pm), another daunting colossus of a museum with 40 galleries. Many offer the press-button joy of working models. Don't miss the beautiful Flight Gallery and the gory reconstructions of operating rooms through the ages in Glimpses of Medical History. South Kensington Station is a short walk across Cromwell Road.

9. Hyde Park *(see map, pages 50–1)*

A morning or afternoon stroll through Hyde Park (at its most animated weekends), starting at the 'last' house in London and then taking in the Serpentine Gallery and the State Apartments at Kensington Palace.

Start at Hyde Park Corner Station (Piccadilly Tube line)

On May Day 1660, Pepys wrote in his diary: 'It being a very pleasant day I wished myself in Hyde Park.' The fact that 300 years later people still have the same idea says much for the enduring attraction of a place in the heart of a changed London.

For the Duke of Wellington it was his back garden. The victor of Waterloo made **Apsley House** (Tues–Sun 11am–5pm) his home from 1817 to his death in 1852; it's the last (or first) house in Piccadilly – No 1 London, as it was known. His architects garnished Robert Adam's brick-built mansion with stone, columns and a portico, but much of the old Adam survives inside in the staircase, drawing room and portico room. Gratitude was heaped on the Duke in the form of plate and porcelain, paintings, some of the spoils of war, sculpture and chandeliers. One gift, 11ft (3.4 metres) high, he

Above: enthralled at the Science Museum
Right: the Albert Memorial

should perhaps have refused – a nude statue of Napoleon that graces the stairwell. Windows face down Rotten Row, the *route du roi* taken by the king from Westminster to the royal hunting forests, and now used for horse riding.

Water Creations in Hyde Park

Hyde Park, where Henry VIII kept his deer and played hide-and-seek with Anne Boleyn, is entered through Decimus Burton's fine screen, a welcoming 'Come on in' from the perils of the traffic at Hyde Park Corner. Serpentine Road, past the bandstand, joins the north bank of the **Serpentine,** created by Queen Caroline in 1830 by damming the Westbourne. George, her husband, would have been cross if he had discovered she had been slipped most of the money to do so by the prime minister! From the bankside beyond the **Dell Café**, look across the water to the Household Cavalry Barracks, which share with the Hilton Hotel responsibility for ruining the park skyline. Between the further bank and the barracks rose the crystal world of the Great International Exhibition of 1851.

Shortly before the bridge is reached, set back against trees on the right and with a formal pool in front, is Jacob Epstein's ***Rima,*** a memorial to the naturalist W. H. Hudson. It was unveiled in 1925 to a tirade of abuse, daubed with green paint and swastikas, but, all passion spent, it survived. The birds, as was intended, like it. Hurry past the fearsome sounding, but rather anonymous Powder Magazine, and enjoy the views from Rennie's beautiful bridge. On its other side is the Lido, where men, women and children can bathe from 6am till dusk in summer.

Cross the road and enter **Kensington Gardens**. You might have been denied the pleasure of access had Queen Caroline had her way and attached the gardens to Kensington Palace. Prime Minister Walpole put her right on the cost – 'Only a Crown, Madam.' The **Serpentine Gallery** (daily 10am–6pm) stages important exhibitions, but for a real jewel look beyond it to William Kent's **Temple Lodge**, then, for a shock contrast in taste, at the **Albert**

Abov and right: Peter Pan and tulips in Kensington Gardens

Memorial, the recently restored jewelled shrine to Victoria's consort. It is a potent, if gaudy, reminder of the ideals and aspirations of the Victorian age.

Diana's Place

Take the Flower Walk to its end in the Broad Walk, then head up to **Kensington Palace** (daily 10am–5pm), inhabited by members of the Royal Family. Princess Diana lived here until her death in 1997 and it has become a place of pilgrimage for her admirers. The fact that the royals now admit visitors to the **State Apartments** and the **Royal Ceremonial Collection** says a lot about the changed character of the monarchy. Kensington Palace had its origins in a private house. After its sale to William III, modest additions were made with the help of Sir Christopher Wren, and later by William Kent for George I.

Just north is the **Orangery** (daily 10am–6pm). Queen Anne liked to have her tea there, and you can too. Another attraction is the sunken 'Dutch' garden near the palace's public entrance. From its surrounding walk, glimpses of the lily pool are framed between bleached lime trees. A path by the south front of the palace crosses the shady Kensington Palace Green. Embassies abound here, often surrounded by interested policemen. Escape can be made to Kensington High Street for buses and the underground.

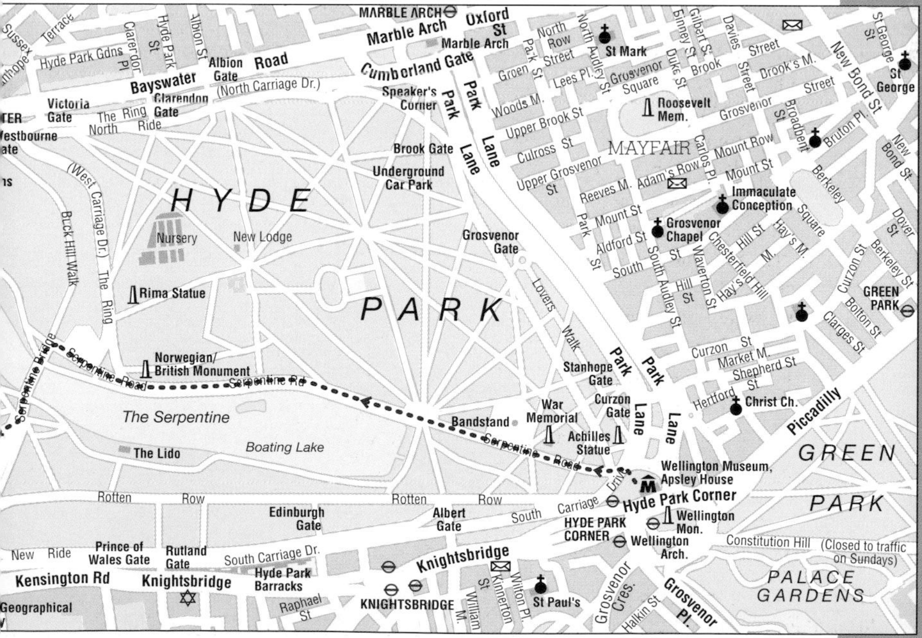

10. Notting Hill *(see map, below)*

Notting Hill's allure comes from its fusion of cultures and lifestyles – Rasta meets pasta, palatial splendour combines with bohemian chic. Come on a Saturday for the market on Portobello Road.

Start at Notting Hill Gate Station (Central, District and Circle Tube lines)

Notting Hill is now the neighbourhood of choice for pop stars and media types: large houses with a W11 postcode will cost at least £1 million. It didn't always have this cachet. In the 1800s, when its grand crescents sat next to noxious slums, it was, according to Dickens, 'a plague spot scarcely equalled for its insalubrity by any other in London'. As recently as the 1950s, the district was very poor. Afro-Caribbeans settled into the overcrowded area in large numbers, resulting in race riots in 1958.

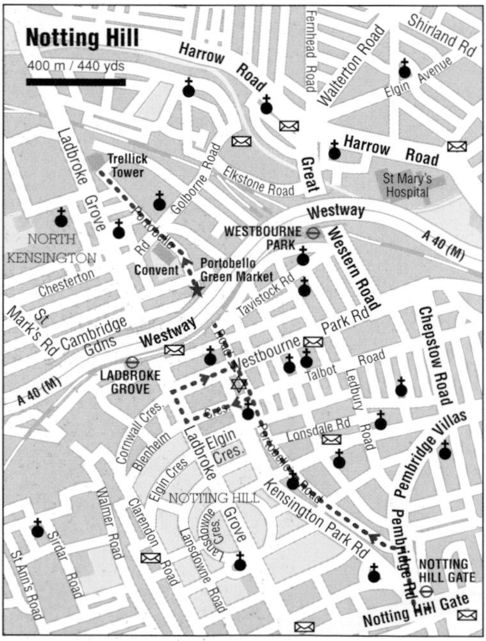

Now different cultures rub along more happily, and the famous Notting Hill Carnival has grown from modest beginnings in the 1960s to be the world's second largest after the carnival in Rio. In 1999, Hollywood gave Notting Hill its stamp of approval with the release of the eponymous film starring Julia Roberts and Hugh Grant. Some lambasted the movie for its unrealistic portrayal because it showed few black people in the neighbourhood.

Above: on Portobello Road

Antiques, Apples, Slippers and Spices

Portobello Road snakes through the heart of the district. When its market began in the 1870s, its dealers were gypsies. Now every Saturday the road becomes a mile of colour and banter. The southern end, starting around Chepstow Villas, is devoted to antiques and collectables – anything from toast racks to teddy bears, and fossils to Ming vases – and bargaining is expected. Dozens of tiny stalls are hidden away in arcades such as the Admiral Vernon.

From **Lonsdale Road**, the theme changes to food. Traditional fruit and veg stalls sit alongside others selling sun-dried tomato and olive breads. Detour left down Blenheim Crescent to **Books for Cooks**, where new recipes are tested on paying guests at lunchtime. Across the road, the Travel Bookshop provided the inspiration for the bookshop in the film *Notting Hill.*

Back on Portobello Road, under the concrete of the Westway flyover, the market gets trendy. Boutiques in **Portobello Green Arcade** are like exotic boudoirs – how about pink heart-shaped sunglasses or a fake fur cardigan? Stalls outside specialise in tie-dyed clothes and bootleg tapes. Beyond the Westway lies a flea market. It peters out in Golborne Road, where Moroccan shops sell slippers and spices, and the large Portuguese community queues for coffee and cakes at **Lisboa**, and dried salted cod, *bacalao*, from the deli opposite. Trellick Tower, looming at the end of the road, was designed by Erno Goldfinger: Ian Fleming named the James Bond villain after him.

If you're starting to feel tired, you can get the Tube at nearby Ladbroke Grove. Otherwise, stay and have lunch at **192**, a quintessentially hip Notting Hill hangout at 192 Kensington Park Road, then wander back to Notting Hill Gate past the 19th-century villas and their communal gardens along Lansdowne Crescent and Lansdowne Road.

11. Regent's Park *(see map, page 54)*

A visit to London Zoo preceded by some of London's finest Regency architecture; then to Queen Mary's Gardens and finally to Madame Tussaud's and the London Planetarium.

Start at Great Portland Street Station (Circle and Metropolitan Tube lines)

Utopian. How else to describe John Nash's conception for the Prince Regent's newly acquired **Marylebone Park**? It was to have a palace, villas for the nobility, terraces of houses for the middle classes, more humble dwellings for the working classes, churches, market and barracks set about a lake, and a river running through a landscaped park. With the exception of the palace, the villas reduced in number from 26 to eight, a single crescent rather than the several planned and the Regent's Canal pressed into service as a river, it's all more or less there.

Get the feel of it by standing on the corner of **Park Crescent**, and imagine the great curve doubled across the Marylebone Road in what would

Right: Regent's Park Crescent

have been Europe's largest circus. Cross the road to Park Square East. In St Andrew's Place is Sir Denys Lasdun's **Royal College of Physicians**, its lecture theatre resembling nothing so much as a surfacing whale. In the Outer Circle, the Victorian Cambridge Gate is on the site of the Colosseum, which at various times housed a panorama of London viewed from St Paul's dome, marine caverns, and an African glen full of stuffed animals. On the left of **Chester Gate** is a small villa and, mounted on the wall, is the bust of a man with 'round head, snub nose, and little eyes' – Nash's description of himself. He omitted the mischievous grin.

View from the Arches

Chester Terrace, long as the Tuileries, is best viewed for its theatrical effect from the park or through the triumphal arches at the ends. Nash and the builder fell out over these. Nash did not want the detached houses that join to the main terrace, but was forced to accept them, finding a happy solution in the triple-arched link. Nash paid special attention to the neighbouring **Cumberland Terrace**, because it would have been the view from the proposed palace, but less to the figures in the pediment, some of which appear to have escaped the overcrowding by taking to the skyline.

Gothic **St Katharine's Hospital** is a refugee from the East End, displaced by the construction of St Katharine's Dock in 1825. Beyond Gloucester Gate turn right and cross Albany Street to **Park Village West**, a village of picturesque villas, especially **Octagon House**, set among gardens on the banks of the now dry canal.

From the village end in Albany Street return to and cross the canal bridge and turn left into Prince Albert Road. Below is the short arm of the canal that led to the **Cumberland Basin** and served the hay market. The heights of **Primrose Hill** (ahead right) give panoramic views over London, but those with less stamina, or with children in tow, may want to turn left over the bridge to the Outer Circle and **London Zoo** (Mar–Sept: daily 10am–5.30pm; Oct–Feb: daily 10am–4pm). The Zoological Society took their bite of the park from the beginning in 1826, and there was some concern that people living there might not like sharing it with lions and leopards. However, its success grew, and in the words of a popular song 'the OK thing to do... is toddle to the Zoo'. Unfortunately zoo-going has become less fashionable, and London Zoo has been kept

afloat by donations from overseas. The best time to visit is feeding time, particularly for the chimpanzees and reptiles.

Tired? A No 274 bus will take you back to Oxford Street, or you can submit to the lure of green space. Take the first opening left beyond the zoo and the second path from the right to cross the bridge over the lake to the Inner Circle. **Queen Mary's Gardens** are the colourful filling in the middle of the circle, with the **Open-Air Theatre** to your left and the café, rose gardens and water gardens on your right.

Opposite is the York Gate entrance to the park and **St Marylebone Church**, borrowed by Nash as an eye-stopper. Go towards Baker Street to see the waxworks brought from Paris by Marie Tussaud in 1802, but don't be surprised if your old-time favourite has been melted down. **Madame Tussaud's** (Mon–Fri 10am–5.30pm, weekends 9.30am–5.30pm, Sun in August 9am–5.30pm) must move with the times if it is to remain London's top attraction (long queues). The **London Planetarium** (Mon–Fri 12.20–5pm, weekends and school holidays 10.20am–5pm) is next door, with shows every 40 minutes. Baker Street Station, on a choice of tube lines, is just beyond.

12. Fleet Street, Inns of Court and Chancery *(see map, page 56)*

To Fleet Street where the pubs remain even if the journalists have gone; try one, then stroll through the Inns of Court and visit the extraordinary Sir John Soane's Museum, then the British Museum.

Ludgate Circus (bus from Charing Cross)

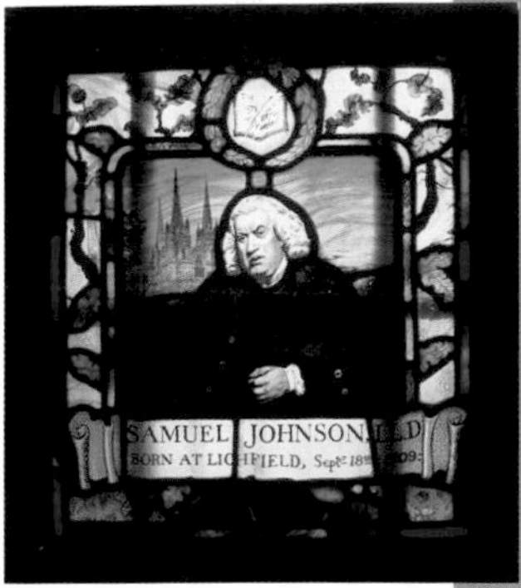

Walk up Fleet Street from Ludgate Circus and you are following the west bank of the old Fleet River, now unceremoniously buried in a sewer. You are also following in the footsteps of generations of journalists and lawyers; the newspapermen have now departed, but the lawyers remain.

On the left, the narrow Bride's Avenue reveals the steeple of **St Bride's church**, Wren's tallest and the inspiration for the first tiered wedding-cake. He rebuilt the church after the Great Fire of London in 1666. It was gutted in the Blitz of 1940, and restored to a new, rather than former, glory. The fascinating **Crypt Museum** (daily 8am–4.45pm) is a magpie col-

Above: getting close to the Fab Four at Madame Tussaud's
Right: Dr Samuel Johnson

lection of Roman mosaics, Saxon church walls and William Caxton's *Ovid*.

Exodus

Across the street, the striking building of black glass and chromium was the brain-centre of Express Newspapers until the 1980s exodus of national newspapers from Fleet Street to cheaper high-tech sites. The pillared palace a few metres further on used to house the *Daily Telegraph*. Look out for **Wine Office Court**, one of the warren of alleys on this side. Here is **Ye Olde Cheshire Cheese** pub (rebuilt 1667), known to Dr Samuel Johnson and his cronies, among them Oliver Goldsmith who lived at No 6. Well-signposted is **Dr Johnson's House** in Gough Square (May–Sept: daily 11am–5.30pm; rest of the year: daily 11am–5pm). Johnson lived here from 1748 to 1759, working on his dictionary in the garret with six poor copyists. Back in Fleet Street, across the road at No 47 is **El Vino's**, a self-important wine bar, once the haunt of self-important journalists and the scene of feminist skirmishes in the 1980s because it wouldn't serve women at the bar (its traditions still dictate that men must wear a tie).

Just beyond Fetter Lane, on the right, is **St Dunstan-in-the-West**, and its 17th-century clock with striking jacks. Over the porch at the side is a lifelike

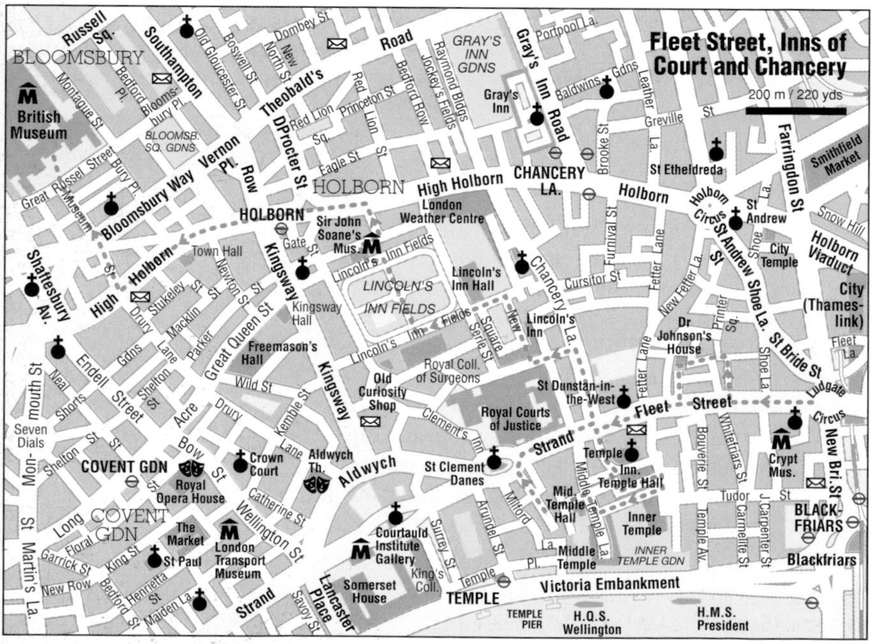

statue of Queen Elizabeth I. When Lud Gate was removed it was brought here together with King Lud and his sons, who loiter in the shadows below. A little further on is the gatehouse entrance to **Clifford's Inn** with the chequered arms of the de Cliffords over the arch, and, beyond, a quiet oasis of trees and grass. **Coutts & Co**. is the bank where Queen Elizabeth II keeps her money. On the south side, at 1 Fleet Street, is **Child & Co**, England's oldest private bank (now part of the Royal Bank of Scotland).

Temple of Law

Just before Child is the half-timbered gateway to Middle Temple Lane and the quadrangles and courts, chambers and gardens of the **Temple**, the heart of legal London. It comprises two of the Inns of Court: the Inner Temple and the Middle Temple. On the first floor of the Inner Temple Gateway of 1611 is **Prince Henry's Room** (Mon–Sat 11am–2pm), with the initials of James I's son on the elaborate ceiling. Enter the lane beneath and turn left for the **Temple Church**, built in 1185 for the Knights Templar.

Head left to King's Bench Walk and turn right in front of Paper Buildings past the gardens running down to the Embankment. In Middle Temple Lane turn right and take the steps left to Fountain Court. Go through the gate to Devereux Court. Turn right from Essex Street to emerge on the Strand, facing the **Royal Courts of Justice**, where England's most important civil law cases are heard. Turn right, then turn into Chancery Lane.

In **Carey Street**, on the left, are the **Silver Mousetrap** jewellers (established 1690) and the **Seven Stars** pub (1602), the 'Magpie and Stump' of Dickens's *Pickwick Papers*. Enter **Lincoln's Inn** through the arch marked New Square. Its aptly-named **Old Hall** was built during the reign of Henry VII. The east gate leads to Lincoln's Inn Fields, the largest square in London.

Sir John Soane's Museum (Tues–Sat 10am–5pm), is at No 13 on the north side of the square. It is a little-publicised gem (and is free), its maze of rooms packed with the 19th-century architect's antiquities and paintings, including Hogarth's *Rake's Progress* and *The Election*. Highly recommended.

This miniature museum serves as an appetiser for the magnificent **British Museum** (Mon–Sat 10am–5pm, Sun 2.30–6pm) located 10 minutes' walk away, It has nearly as many visitors each year (over 5½ million) as objects in its collection (over 6½ million). Many of its famous antiquities were pilfered from the sites of the world's great ancient civilisations, making the museum's name something of a misnomer. The Greek government has demanded the return of the Elgin Marbles, and it is expected that a number of items will be returned to their place of origin.

You could explore the British Museum for days; but, if pressed, don't miss the Elgin Marbles, the Anglo-Saxon jewellery from the Sutton Hoo ship burial and the Egyptian mummies. The museum's fascinating manuscripts are now in the **British Library** next to St Pancras Station on Euston Road.

Above left: an architect's library, Sir John Soane's Museum. **Right:** exhibit in the British Museum

13. St Paul's and Smithfield (see map, opposite)

St Paul's, Christopher Wren's magnificent cathedral; Smithfield Meat Market; London's oldest hospital; medieval alleys, and Karl Marx's Memorial Library.

Start at St Paul's Station (Central Tube line)

On 29 December 1940 **St Paul's Cathedral** held its breath. A year into World War II it was ringed with fire as bombs rained down on the heart of London. Miraculously it survived, a symbol of a nation's resistance. The spire of its Gothic predecessor had succumbed to fire in 1561, and upkeep deteriorated. Inigo Jones gave the west front a face-lift, but the Great Fire of London hastened the decision to rebuild, with Wren embarking on a plan in 1672. His magnificent wooden model was rejected and the end result was a compromise.

Return to Newgate Street and head along it until you reach the Central Criminal Court, or **Old Bailey**, where the country's most important criminal trials are held. Take Giltspur Street to West Smithfield, which has seen public executions and burnings, the slaughter of cattle, and St Bartholomew's Fair, which foundered on vice and violence in 1840. At the ringside are London's oldest hospital, St Bartholomew's, and its oldest church, St Bartholomew-the-Great, both founded on humanitarian and religious ideals by Henry I's jester, Rahere.

Good Works of St Bartholomew

Bart's Gatehouse, with Henry VIII in a niche, looks more like the entrance to a college quad than a hospital. Walk through to see, on the left, the hos-

Top: St Paul's Cathedral at dusk
Above: the gatehouse of Charterhouse

pital church, **St Bartholomew-the-Less**, a Gothic octagon of 1823 sitting happily with a medieval tower. Outside, turn right to the 13th-century arch of the gatehouse to **St Bartholomew-the-Great**, its half-timbering hidden until a World War I bomb revealed all. Enter the church and you are in the Norman chancel of the demolished nave of the Augustinian Priory. Prior Bolton's oriel window high in the south side enabled him to drop in on proceedings unobserved.

No 41 Cloth Fair, overlooking the graveyard, gives a good idea of what London looked like before the Great Fire. John Betjeman described his house on the corner opposite as 'the nicest place to live in' before the night-time roar of the trucks drove him out. A little further on a passage takes you to Long Lane and **Ye Olde Red Cow**, home of 'Hot Toddy'. Early starts for porters at **Smithfield Meat Market** – the giant Victorian warehouse across the street – mean the local pubs open at 5.30am. If you want to see the market in action, you need to get there at 9am at the latest.

Cross to Lindsey Street and Charterhouse Square. The **Charterhouse** (Apr–Jul: Wed tour at 2.15pm), first a Carthusian Priory founded in 1371, became a manor house for the Duke of Norfolk, and, later, coal-owner Thomas Sutton's 'hospital' for poor brethren (a school for poor boys), then a public school. Now 'gentlemen pensioners' live there.

Jerusalem in the East End

Turn right into St John Street, fork left into St John's Lane and walk back 400 years to the Gatehouse of the Priory of St John of Jerusalem. Elizabeth I's Master of Revels had his office here and the *Gentleman's Magazine* used to be published here. Cross Clerkenwell Road to St John's Square, once the courtyard of the priory. Jerusalem Passage leads to Aylesbury Street and Clerkenwell Green. At the end of the Green is the elegant, restored **Old Sessions House**, built in 1782. The good **Crown** pub has a Conspirators' Clock in the bar, commemorating the unsuccessful attempt on the life of Charles II.

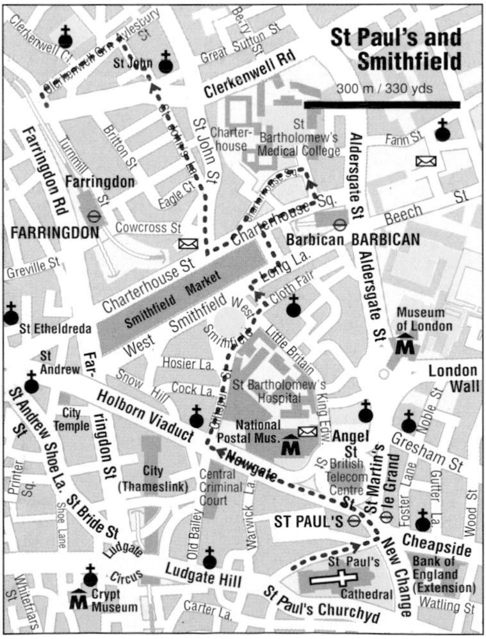

Facing the Green is the **Marx Memorial Library** (Mon 1–6pm, Tues–Thurs 1–8pm, Sat 10am–1pm) at No 37a. In 1892 the first socialist press was set up in this building, and in a tiny corner office, Lenin edited *Iskra*, 'The Spark', that was to kindle the Russian Revolution. When you are ready to leave the area, Farringdon Station is left down Farringdon Road.

Excursions

1. HAMPSTEAD *(see pull-out map)*

A stroll around the hilly Georgian 'village' of Hampstead, ending with a tramp across London's most invigorating park, Hampstead Heath.

Underground to Hampstead Station (Northern Tube line)

For writers, painters, and anyone of a liberal disposition, Hampstead has long been the place to live. At the last count, there were more than 90 blue plaques on houses commemorating famous residents – from John Constable to George Orwell, and Florence Nightingale to Sigmund Freud. Now you also need to have deep pockets to live here: with its pretty alleys, leafy backstreets and the heath on its doorstep, the suburb has become one of London's most desirable districts.

From the Tube, take Heath Street down to Church Row, which has Hampstead's best display of Georgian architecture. Follow the sign to John Constable's grave in the bosky graveyard of St John's Church, halfway along the row. Then take Holly Walk, past the one-time home of Robert Louis Stevenson, up to Hampstead Grove. **Fenton House** (Mar–Oct: Wed–Fri 2–5pm, weekends 11am–5pm), the grand William and Mary mansion behind gilded gates, has fascinating antique musical instruments. Return to Hampstead Grove, descend the steps down to Heath Street, and cross over down New End. **Burgh House** (daily noon–5pm), at the far end of the street, dates from the late 17th century, when Hampstead was turning into a fashionable spa town. Now it's a good local history museum, with maps showing the location of 166 homes of celebrated residents, and a permanent display on Constable.

Flask Walk becomes a pedestrian alleyway of arty shops just before it reaches the High Street. Follow the High Street to Downshire Hill, a beautiful street of Regency houses. The modernist **2 Willow Road** (Apr–Oct: Thur–Sat noon–5pm), overlooking the heath, was designed by Erno Goldfinger, and is filled with the architect's outstanding modern art. John Keats lodged in a Regency villa around the corner on what is now called Keats' Grove, during which time he penned one of his best-loved poems, *Ode to a Nightingale*. **Keats' House** (Mon–Fri 10am–1pm and 2–6pm, Sat 10am–1pm and 2–5pm, Sun 2–5pm) is a little lifeless, but contains a number of moving keepsakes of Fanny Brawne, the neighbour with whom he fell in love.

Left: neoclassical Kenwood House
Right: Hampstead High Street

The meadows, woods and heathland of **Hampstead Heath** are as rural as London gets. Climb **Parliament Hill** for superlative views across the capital, then strike north to **Kenwood House** (summer: daily 10am–6pm; winter: daily 10am–4pm). The Adam mansion, overlooking parkland, holds a fine collection of 17th- and 18th-century art. Nearby, at the northern end of Spaniards Road, is the **Spaniard's Inn**, a cosy 16th-century coaching inn once frequented by highwayman Dick Turpin. Hampstead tube station is a 15-minute walk back down the hill.

2. Kew Gardens *(see pull-out map)*

With its giant Victorian glasshouses, eccentric follies and 300 acres/121 hectares of landscaped grounds, Kew Gardens appeals not only to keen horticulturalists.

Take the riverboat from Westminster Pier (Easter–Oct; journey time 90 minutes; tel: 020-7930 2062 for departure times) or take the District Tube line to Kew Gardens

Kew Gardens' official name is the **Royal Botanic Gardens** (summer: Mon–Fri 9.30am–6.30pm, weekends till 7.30pm; winter: 9.30am–dusk). Prince Frederick, son of George II, created a royal pleasure garden here in 1731, but it was his widow, Augusta, who introduced the botanical element in 1759. The gardens became famous after botanist Sir Joseph Banks returned in 1771 from his global travels with Captain Cook, recording then unknown plants, many of which he introduced at Kew. Meanwhile, the grounds were landscaped by William Chambers and 'Capability' Brown.

There are now an astonishing 30,000 different types of plants grown here. Any time of year is good to visit. In February you'll see carpets of crocuses and snowdrops, in May bluebells and azeleas, in June rhododendrons, in autumn a kaleidoscope of arboreal colour. Some of the most interesting specimens are on show year-round in the glasshouses.

If you come by river, it's a five-minute walk from the pier to Main Gate. If you arrive by tube, Victoria Gate (confusingly the main entrance) is just a couple of minutes' walk away. Consider bringing a picnic; otherwise the

most enjoyable café is the grand 18th-century **Orangery**. You can start your visit by taking the new trolley service around the gardens for an overview: it leaves from Victoria Gate every hour.

Steamy Rainforest

The star attraction of Kew is the **Palm House**, a curvaceous glasshouse built in 1848. Inside, spiral wrought-iron stairs climb up through the steamy rain-forest sections to galleries. Just behind lies the **Waterlily House**, its circular pond covered in giant Amazonian lilies. Two other glasshouses are not to be missed. The **Temperate House** took the Victorians 40 years to complete and is on an awesome scale. Though less aesthetically pleasing, the modern **Princess of Wales Conservatory** is divided into 10 micro-climates suitable for everything from cacti to carnivorous plants. Walking from one section to another is like going in and out of a sauna. Beyond the glasshouses, chart your route according to the season – and look out for quirky follies, such as the tapering 9-storey pagoda, and a neoclassical temple.

3. Greenwich *(see pull-out map)*

A trip down the river to the 'village' of Greenwich for the Maritime Museum, Royal Observatory and Millennium Dome.

Take a boat from Westminster, Charing Cross or Embankment piers, or the Docklands Light Railway to Cutty Sark

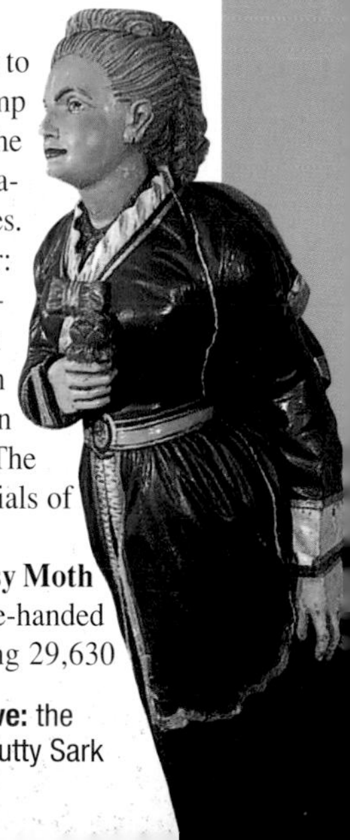

Queen Elizabeth I took her state barge from Whitehall Stairs to be rowed downstream to her palace at Greenwich. With less pomp and more comfort, a boat from central London will take you to the country's finest group of royal buildings, successors to Elizabeth's Tudor retreat built by Sir Christopher Wren and Inigo Jones.

Alongside Greenwich Pier is the **Cutty Sark** (summer: Mon–Sat 10am–6pm, Sun noon–6pm; winter till 5pm), a greyhound of clippers that carried China tea and, later, Australian wool from her launch in Scotland in 1869 to her retirement in 1922 – the last and the fastest. The article of underwear worn by the lady on the prow is a Scottish nightshirt, a 'cutty sark'. The clipper now carries a cargo of superb figureheads, the memorials of a vanished fleet.

Dwarfed in size, though not in terms of achievement, is **Gipsy Moth IV**. In 1966–7 Sir Francis Chichester was the first to sail single-handed round the world in this ketch, achieved in 226 days, covering 29,630

Left: Kew Palace, inside the gardens, is also open to the public. **Above:** the Waterlily House at Kew. **Right:** one of the figureheads on board the Cutty Sark

miles (47,685km). Nearby is the entrance to the Foot Tunnel which leads under the river to the Isle of Dogs. After a cold trudge through the tunnel you are rewarded by an unsurpassed view of Greenwich, the 'Queen's View', from the other side. If you don't fancy the walk you can hop on the Docklands Light Railway for one stop to Island Gardens.

Back by the pier on the Greenwich side, the riverside walk passes the two blocks of the Royal Naval College, with a gap between to ensure the Queen's unobstructed view of the river from Queen's House, and ends by the Regency **Trafalgar Tavern**, where Cabinet ministers came for whitebait dinners. Continue ahead, past the Yacht, the Trinity Almshouses, founded in 1613, and the power station, to the riverside, and the Georgian **Cutty Sark** pub, which looks as if it was built of ships' timbers. From here there are views of Greenwich Reach and the Millennium Dome.

Back at Park Row, cross Romney Road to the National Maritime Museum. A colonnaded walk links the west and east wings with the recently-restored **Queen's House** (daily 10am–5pm), on the line of the old Dover Road which tunnels beneath Inigo Jones's building. This, England's first Palladian villa, was intended for James I's Queen Anne, but was only completed after her death, by Charles I for Henrietta Maria. Tiptoe up beside the beautiful wrought-iron balustrade on the Tulip Staircase.

The displays of the **National Maritime Museum** (daily 10am–5pm) are housed in the west wing. It has recently undergone a £20 million transformation to turn it into one of London's best-presented museums, and goes far beyond what you might expect from its title. Don't miss the Royal Barge of 1732, designed by William Kent with a riot of lions, dragons and scaly

Top: entrance to the Royal Naval College
Above: Greenwich Mean Time

monsters. Nelson has a whole, fascinating gallery dedicated to himself, with the very tunic he was wearing when he was fatally wounded at Trafalgar (you can see the musket ball hole).

Wren's Naval College

From the Romney Road exit turn right in King William Walk into the **Royal Naval College** (daily 2.30–5pm), which occupies the site of the Tudor Palace. Here, Cromwell's sense of history appears to have deserted him. During the Commonwealth he allowed the palace to serve as a biscuit factory for his troops in Scotland. Not until 1694 was Wren approached to design not a palace, but a hospital for elderly and sick seamen. The Royal Naval College came here from Portsmouth in 1873, and only the Painted Hall in King William Block and the Chapel in Queen Mary Block are open to the public. The splendour of the architecture is matched by Thornhill's decoration of the **Painted Hall**, which was begun in 1707, but not completed until 1726. The **Chapel** dates from 1742, but was rebuilt by James 'Athenian' Stuart after an extensive fire.

Opposite the College is the **Covered Market**, now given over to arts and crafts. Where St Alfege's Church puts on a bold front to the street, turn left past Greenwich Theatre, a phoenix that has risen from the shell of an old music hall, into Croom's Hill. Among the hill's fine 17th- and 18th-century houses is a Wren-style gazebo of 1672.

Keep left along Chesterfield Walk for the **Ranger's House** (Apr–Oct: daily 10am–6pm; Nov–Mar: Wed–Sun 10am–1pm and 2–4pm), which was once the home of Lord Chesterfield; it has portraits downstairs and the Dolmetsch Collection of musical instruments above.

Behind the house, bear left through glorious **Greenwich Park** – a royal hunting ground until the 18th century – for the **Old Royal Observatory** (daily 10am–5pm). Charles II founded it in 1675. Wren, an astronomer himself, designed it for Flamsteed, the Astronomer Royal, who lived under the shop just as his successors did until polluted London air drove them away. Greenwich Time was universally accepted in 1884 with the establishment of the **Meridian**, and East meets West in the brass strip on the path. Every day at 1pm a time-ball drops on the turret mast. If you happen to be outward bound on the river below, you can check your chronometer.

Given Greenwich's significance in the history of time, it was not accidental that it was chosen as the focus for Britain's millennium festivities. Return to Greenwich Pier, from where you can take either a shuttle bus or boat downriver to the **Millennium Dome**. Covering a 20-acre (100-hectare) site, it is said to be the largest exhibition structure in the world. Ever since the project began in 1996, the Dome has been plagued by controversy – hardly surprising given that it has cost £750 million and the building has only a

Right: the Millennium Dome

25-year lifespan, though over 12 million visitors are expected in the year 2000. Under the upturned bowl you will find the **Millennium Experience** (tickets must be purchased in advance, from newsagents that also sell Lottery tickets or by phone, tel: 0870 606 2000; exhibition will close at the end of 2000). A glorified theme park, it's divided into 14 zones (for example Body, Mind, Faith) that celebrate British ideas and technology, and examine how we are dealing with life at the outset of the 21st century.

4. HAMPTON COURT PALACE *(see pull-out map)*

By river or train to the great 16th-century palace of Hampton Court; get lost in the maze, and see the splendour in which Cardinal Wolsey and Henry VIII passed their days.

Hampton Court Station by train from Waterloo (30 minutes); or boat trip from Westminster Pier (Easter–Oct; journey time 3 hours; tel: 020-7930 2062 for departure times)

From the Landing Stage a short path leads to the moat bridge, but the best approach is through the **Trophy Gates** (mid-Mar–mid-Oct: Tues–Sun 9.30am–6pm, Mon 10.15am–6pm; rest of the year: Tues–Sun 9.30am–4.30pm, Mon 10.15am–4.30pm). Here the scale and complexity of the great Tudor palace with its forest of chimneys and turrets is at its most impressive, but this is only one side of the coin. Behind lies Sir Christopher Wren's contribution, which invites comparison with Versailles.

Cardinal Wolsey, the butcher's son who rose to the highest offices in the Church (with a town house in Whitehall which later became a palace) bought the manor in 1514 and built himself a country seat of such magnificence as to raise the envy of Henry VIII. Too late, Wolsey offered it to him as a sweetener, only to have all his possessions taken from him. A year after being charged with treason he was dead. Wolsey's **Great Gatehouse**, originally two storeys higher, rises over a dry moat and a bridge

built by Henry VIII, only excavated in recent times. Charles II had 'improved' them out of existence. **Base Court** is all Wolsey and built of plummy red brick. Behind the mullioned windows are some of the 280 rooms he kept prepared for guests. The medallions were made by Giovanni da Maiano – eight for a 1521 pound. The stone roof of **Anne Boleyn's Gateway** has Henry and Anne's initials in lovers' knots.

'Modern' embellishments

In **Clock Court** is the Astronomical Clock made by Nicholas Oursian in 1540. Henry's **Great Hall** fills one side of the court; at its end is possibly the finest example of an oriel window in England. On the south side is Wren's colonnade, as contrasting to the Tudor as the glass pyramid is to the Louvre. To complete this trip through time, the east side with the gateway was remodelled by William Kent in 1732 in his own idea of revived Gothic. Wolsey's and Henry's buildings bring a nice domestic feel to the north range of the palace. It is somehow easier to catch the spirit of the time in the **Wine Cellar** and the **Kitchens**, where serving places, stairs and the Horn Room separated them from table in the Great Hall. There Shakespeare and his Company of Players may well have entertained Queen Elizabeth I. Our only view of the **Chapel Royal** is from the Royal Pew, where Henry VIII heard Mass oblivious of piercing screams from his wife Catherine Howard in the nearby gallery. After her death, the appearance of a figure in white and the sounds of unearthly shrieks gained it the title of the Haunted Gallery. It is something of a relief to turn to the **Wolsey Rooms**, and his sitting room in particular with its beautiful decoration and panelling.

Fountain Court reflects Wren's intention to rebuild the whole palace for William and Mary. Begun in 1685, only the east and south fronts were completed. The grandeur is somehow lacking, but you can relate to Hampton Court where Versailles intimidates. Grand staircases lead to the **King's and Queen's Apartments**, ornamented with Verrio's painting, Gibbons's carving and Tijou's ironwork. Among other delights are the gardens, which include the **Great Vine** that can still astonish after more than 200 years, the formal **Privy Gardens**, and the solution-defying **Maze**. As Harris said in Jerome K. Jerome's *Three Men in a Boat*, 'We'll just walk round for ten minutes and then go and get some lunch.' Be advised: have lunch first. The **Tiltyard Restaurant** is nearby or, in Hampton Court Road opposite the Trophy Gates, the **Liongate** and **The King's Arms** pubs.

Return to the pier for a Richmond boat, or cross the bridge to the station for trains to Waterloo.

Left: the Privy Gardens at the back of Hampton Court Palace
Right: the Palace entrance

Whistles

Leisure Activities

SHOPPING

London is a consumer's paradise – even if prices are not always competitive by the standards set in stores in the United States and some European countries. The best times to search for bargains, especially in the big department stores, are during the winter and summer sales in January and July. In many shops, visitors from non-European Union countries can claim back the 17.5 percent Value Added Tax (VAT) levied on most goods – always automatically included in the price – provided they have paid a significant price for them. Ask the shop for a form and give it to Customs on leaving the country.

If you want a detailed guide to the best of shopping in London, buy the annual *Time Out London Shopping Guide*. Below, we've divided shopping into different areas, each with its own markedly individual character. For shopping hours, see page 87.

Oxford Street and Regent Street

Oxford Street is England's principal high street and is always crowded. The western end, between Oxford Circus and Marble Arch, is its smarter half; the eastern end leads into Tottenham Court Road, a centre for electronic goods and furniture stores, including **Heal's**, selling quality modern furniture. Oxford Street has all the major high street fashion chains such as **Gap** and **Benetton**. There are also large branches of **Virgin** and **HMV Records**, a dazzling new **Niketown** sports shop on Oxford Circus, and several department stores, of which **Selfridge's**, built by the American Gordon Selfridge and opened in 1909, is the grandest. **John Lewis** stocks conservative ranges, but is equally vast and always good value – it prides itself on its 'never knowingly undersold' policy. The Marble Arch Branch of **Marks & Spencer** is the flagship of this leading British chain store with its own brand of quality, inexpensive clothes for the whole family.

Left: for sale in Covent Garden
Right: Burlington Arcade

Opposite Bond Street Tube is a discreet little alleyway leading to St Christopher's Place where a cluster of trendy shops have grouped together. On the other side of Oxford Street is South Molton Street which moves in the direction of Bond Street both geographically and in its range of up-market boutiques. Stores such as **Browns** stock collections from major international designers.

Serious shopping along Regent Street begins at Oxford Circus with **Dickins & Jones**, a classy fashion store for mature tastes. Next door is the mock Tudor frontage of **Liberty**, famous for its exquisite printed fabrics, but also with good designer womenswear, a perfumerie and furniture department. Nearby, **Hamley's** proclaims itself to be the world's largest toy shop, extending over 7 floors. Towards Piccadilly are more child-oriented shops, **The Disney Store**, **Warner Brothers Studio Store** and **Lego Kids**. Also here are upmarket jewellers and fine china shops such as **Waterford, Wedgwood** and **Royal Doulton**. **Jaeger**, **Austin Reed** and **Aquascutum** are good for classic English clothes and country casuals.

Bond Streeet and Mayfair

Bond Street has a long-standing tradition of offering the best money can buy, and if any of London's streets are paved with gold it must surely be this one. In this vicinity are

more than 400 of the world's most élite fine art and antique galleries, plus leading auction houses, exquisite jewellers such as **Tiffany**, **Cartier** and **Georg Jenson**, and leading international couturiers, **Valentino**, **Chanel**, **Lagerfeld**, **Donna Karan** and **Nicole Fahri** among others. The southern end of New Bond Street is wall-to-wall jewellers. **Asprey & Garrard**, with the royal seal of approval, is very English and specialises in antique silver. Running parallel to Old Bond Street is the elegant Burlington Arcade (see Walk 3: *West End*), lined with small exclusive shops, many selling quality British-made goods.

St James's and Piccadilly

This area, which is littered with gentlemen's clubs, is steeped in tradition and the 'old order'. Here is a concentration of old-fashioned gentlemen's outfitters with the hand-tailored suits of Savile Row and the made-to-measure shirts of Jermyn Street. In timeless St James's Street are shoemaker **John Lobb** and fine hat maker **James Lock**, whilst in Jermyn Street, **George F Trumper** supplies traditional toiletries to the aristocracy and **Floris** provides them with wonderful fragrances.

The Dickensian wine merchants **Berry Bros & Rudd** at 3 St James's Street have a cellar stocked with rare wines, while **JJ Fox** and **Davidoff** have the perfect accompaniment – prized, fat Havana cigars. **Fortnum & Mason** on Piccadilly have been supplying the English gentry with exotic and unusual groceries for centuries; the prices are double what you'd pay in the supermarket, but the quality of the food, the shop's ambience and the tail-coated staff more than compensate. For the traditional English look, **Simpson** at 203 Piccadilly has several floors of fine clothing for men and women. **Lillywhite's**, on Piccadilly Circus, has the widest range of sports goods in London.

Knightsbridge

Harrods, on Brompton Road, dominates the scene of exclusive and high fashion shopping in Knightsbridge. It is one of the world's largest and most famous department stores, with 300 departments and 4,000 staff. No-one should miss the fabulous displays in the Edwardian tiled food halls, where you can buy anything from indulgent hampers to melons carved to your own design. Close by is **Harvey Nichols**, known as Harvey Nicks, where anyone who is anyone comes to shop for the latest in designer clothes. Round the corner, the top end of Sloane Street has become a centre for high fashion too, with many world-class designers here. Beauchamp Place is prettier, friendlier and quirkier – a mix of chichi clothes bou-

tiques and shops specialising in antique maps or upmarket comestibles such as Umbrian truffles.

King's Road and Fulham

Despite rising overheads, which have caused many of the distinctive independent boutiques to disappear, the King's Road is still good for trendy street fashion. At the Sloane Square end is Chelsea's only department store, **Peter Jones**, particularly good for household furnishings and appliances at unbeatable prices; at the other end – the hipper World's End end – is Vivienne Westwood's wacky store with its rapidly whirling clocks (No 430). A stroll from west to east should take in **American Classics** (No 398) for second-hand US clothing, the avant garde shoe designer **Johnny Moke** next door, and **Timney Fowler** (No 388) for chic soft furnishings. Continue on to **Bluebird** at No 350, arguably the most mouthwatering deli-cum-food-hall in London, created by Terence Conran out of a listed garage. He would probably approve of most of the individual pieces of furniture and gorgeous fabrics in the **Designer's Guild** at No 267. **Daisy & Tom**, at No 181, is the neighbourhood's favourite toy shop, a couple of notches more civilised than Hamley's: there is a good kiddie-oriented café and even a child-makeover service. **Antiquarius**, at Nos 131–41, is the best one-stop shop for antiques on the road: this fascinating centre has over 120 dealers. For a one-stop shop for designer gear, consider **The Common Market** at No 121; the **Joseph Sale Shop** at No 53 offers great bargains.

It's worth also making a detour up to the north end of Fulham Road for **The Conran Shop**, housed within the beautiful Art Nouveau-tiled Michelin building at No 81, and bursting with desirable household objects – yours, at a price.

Kensington

Although largely inhabited by chain stores, Kensington High Street is still good for mainstream fashion. An oddity is **Kensington Market** (Nos 49–53), full of stalls selling leather jackets and all the latest club gear. Away from the hustle and bustle of the High Street is Kensington Church Street with some of London's finest, and most expensive, antique shops, dealing in everything from fine art originals through to oriental rugs and European porcelain.

Covent Garden and Soho

Within the narrow streets and piazzas of this characterfully redeveloped area, many interesting craft and gift shops and stalls have taken root. Covent Garden, once London's main fruit and vegetable market, also offers the designer wear of **Nicole Farhi**, **Agnes B**, **Paul Smith**, **Jones** (all on Floral Street) and **Michiko Koshino**, as well as leading fashion chains such as **Jigsaw**, **Whistles**, **Hobbs**, **Woodhouse** and **Blazer**. Several good, though rather expensive, period clothes shops can be found around Neal Street and Monmouth Street.

The quaint **Neal's Yard** is a centre for organic wholefood. Opposite Neal's Yard is a smart new shopping centre, **Thomas Neal's**.

On Long Acre is **Stanford's**, offering the largest selection of maps and travel books (guides and literature), and next-door **Dillons Art Bookshop**, covering all aspects of art, design and architecture. Nearby, Charing Cross Road is a haven for bookworms. It is crowded with bookshops ranging from **Foyles**, the largest and most labyrinthine, to better laid-out stores such as the nearby **Waterstone's** and **Borders**, and the small antiquarian establishments nestling in Cecil Court, a little pedestrian street on the way towards Trafalgar Square.

Much of the sleaze of old Soho has been swept away to be replaced by wild and trendy fashion shops. Despite Carnaby Street's downhill spiral following the 'swinging Sixties', a spirit of innovation still flourishes in its neighbouring lanes such as Newburgh Street and Fouberts Place. More mainstream clothes (**Jigsaw**, **Laura Ashley**, **French Connection**) are found in Argyll Street.

Several old Italian delicatessens such as **Camisa & Son** in Old Compton Street and **Lina Stores** in Brewer Street are still standing their ground – and selling delicious cheeses, hams and porcini mushrooms – survivors of an era when Soho was far more continental. Meanwhile, Chinatown, which is centred around Gerrard Street, is the obvious place for the best Chinese groceries.

Left: entertaining the shoppers at Covent Garden

Markets

For everything from antiques, bric-à-brac and period clothes to general junk and fruit and veg, make for **Portobello Road** *(see page 53)* on Sat 8am–6pm, which is effectively several markets rolled into one. The fruit and veg stalls are also open Mon–Friday, and the clothes and junk Friday and Sunday. Many antique dealers do their shopping here, so the stall-holders know what they are selling, and the prices reflect this. Antiques browsers should also head for pretty, small-scale **Camden Passage** N1 – confusingly in Islington not Camden – on Wed and Sat 8am–4pm, and the market in **Bermondsey Square** SE1 on Fri 5am–2pm, which deals in small items and is geared to the serious trader.

Camden Market NW1, is the biggest and most visited in London. Much of it is aimed at a young crowd in search of second-hand clothes, crafts, hip jewellery and records. It divides into half a dozen areas, the most popular being Camden Lock (daily 10am– 6pm), which, like the whole market, is incredibly busy at weekends.

Brick Lane E1 (Sun 8am–1pm) couldn't be more different than Camden Market. It is dishevelled and disorganised, and oozing with East End atmosphere; goods are cheap, many having probably 'fallen off the back of a lorry'. **Columbia Road** E2 (Sun 8am– 1pm), a short walk away, is one of London's most colourful markets, devoted to plants and flowers. **Petticoat Lane**, around Middlesex Street E1 (Sun 9am–2pm) is far more touristy than Brick Lane, and always packed, but it's a good hunting ground for budget clothes, especially leather goods. **Greenwich Market** (weekends 9am–5pm) is a relaxed, browser's paradise, with antiques, second-hand books, crafts, etc., sold in the attractive covered market and surrounding streets.

For food, **Berwick Street** W1 *(see page 24)* is a bustling weekday market (Mon–Sat 8am–6pm) selling high-quality fruit and veg at good prices. **Leadenhall** EC3 *(see page 37)* in a beautiful Victorian covered (lead-roofed) market hall, has been gentrified and is good for quality meat, poultry and fish (Mon–Fri 7am–4pm). **Brixton Market** SW9, (Mon–Sat 8am–6pm) comprises a street market along Electric Avenue and a permanent covered market, both offering wonderfully exotic produce stalls catering to the area's Afro-Caribbean community.

Of the wholesale markets, Billingsgate, described as being the home of fresh fish and foul language, moved to Docklands, but **Smithfield Meat Market** EC1 (Mon–Fri 5–10.30am, *see page 59*), has stayed put, and welcomes visitors who don't get in the way. **Spitalfield** EC1, formerly a massive fruit and veg market, has been transformed into a trendy organic market (Fri–Sun 10am–5pm) and has also turned its hand to selling crafts (daily except Sat).

Above: browsing through books in Petticoat Lane market

EATING OUT

London has become one of the great culinary cities of the world. This is partly due to the breadth of cosmopolitan cuisines available, but also to the re-evaluation over recent years of the indigenous cuisine of the British. Innovative chefs have injected new life into traditional English recipes, enriching them with French and ethnic influences. However, the traditional Sunday lunch, roast carveries and fish and chips are still very much part of the scene, as is 'afternoon tea', which is served in many hotels.

Restaurants in central London are especially concentrated in the West End, with Soho providing the most interesting and widest choice, whilst Covent Garden can offer good pre-theatre suppers. Chinatown, centring on Gerrard Street, is full of Cantonese restaurants. Bayswater also has many good value ethnic restaurants.

A good meal out in London can be expensive; however, many restaurants – including some of the top ones – provide cheaper set-price menus at lunchtime. Ethnic restaurants are some of the best value, and pubs, wine bars and cafés often serve good, inexpensive snacks. If you are counting the pennies, you can't go far wrong with a take-away English fish and chips. Restaurant Services (020-8888 8080) give up-to-date, impartial information and also provide a free booking service.

At establishments described below as expensive, expect to pay over £90 for a three-course dinner for two people, including a bottle of house wine and a tip; for those listed as moderate, prepare to pay £50–90, and for inexpensive restaurants under £50. You will need to book well in advance to secure a table at most of the following restaurants, especially for dining on Thursday, Friday and Saturday evenings; some restaurants offer two-hour sittings, say from 7pm or 9pm .

Traditional British

The Quality Chop House
94 Farringdon Road, EC1
Tel: 020-7837 5093
A 19th-century City clerks' dining room with original fixed wooden seating intact. Food ranging from blue fish with fennel sauce to plain lamb chops. Moderate.

Rules
35 Maiden Lane, WC2
Tel: 020 7836 5314
Over 200 years old, with a long-established literary clientele. Game in season, and old-fashioned puddings such as treacle sponge and custard. Moderate–expensive.

Simpsons-in-the-Strand
100 Strand, WC2
Tel: 020-7836 9112
The Grand Divan Tavern is an Edwardian dining room renowned for serving the best roast beef in London. Staunchly traditional. Formal dress. Expensive.

Modern British

Alastair Little
49 Frith Street, W1
Tel: 020-7734 5183
Doyen of the new school of British cooking: imaginative and eclectic food within tasteful surroundings. Moderate–expensive.

Andrew Edmunds
46 Lexington Street, W1
Tel: 020-7437 5708
Long-established and informal, cosy and candlelit, this Soho restaurant is a welcome antidote to its flashier, fly-by-night competitors. Moderate.

Blue Print Café
Design Museum, Butler's Wharf, SE1
Tel: 020-7378 7031
The first of Terence Conran's many London restaurant ventures has fantastic views over the Thames. Delicious British/Mediterranean creations to the fore. Moderate.

The Eagle
159 Farringdon Road, EC1
Tel: 020-7837 1353
Said to be the first of the many 'gastro-pubs' now found in London. It's busy, noisy and crowded, and the British-Iberian food is excellent. No reservations. Inexpensive.

Mash
19–21 Great Portland Street, W1
Tel: 020-7637 5555
Ultra-modern restaurant with a bar and brewery downstairs that is very popular with a

young crowd. Creative twists to Mediterranean fare. The loos offer something of a surprise. Moderate.

Mezzo
100 Wardour Street, W1
Tel: 020-7314 4000
One of Terence Conran's restaurants. Vast in size and very fashionable. Mediterranean-influenced food. Glamorous. Moderate; also a cheaper café.

Quaglino's
16 Bury Street, SW1
Tel: 020-7930 6767
An expansive, theatrical see-and-be-seen dining-room serving high-quality, modern brasserie fare. Moderate–expensive.

Union Café
96 Marylebone Lane, W1
Tel: 020-7486 4860
Imaginative twists on traditional favourites. Moderate.

American Theme

Hard Rock Café
150 Old Park Lane, W1
Tel: 020-7629 0382
Part of the world-wide chain. A shrine to rock music, housing a collection of rock memorabilia. Serves good burgers. Noisy with long queues but great fun. No reservations. Inexpensive.

Belgian

Belgo Centraal
50 Earlham Street, WC2
Tel: 020-7813 2233
Good beer, excellent mussels and *frites* and other Belgian dishes, served by waiters dressed as monks in an industrial-style cellar. Inexpensive.

Chinese

Fung Shing
15 Lisle Street, W1
Tel: 020-7437 1539
This has long been one of the best restaurants in Chinatown, and it's always packed. If it is full, there are plenty of other choices nearby. Moderate.

Fish

Fish!
Cathedral Street, Borough Market, SE1
Tel: 020-7836 3236
Lively, glass-sided Victorian pavilion in the shadow of Southwark Cathedral, serving the freshest of fish in refreshingly simple dishes. Better atmosphere at lunchtime. Moderate.

Livebait
43 The Cut, SE1
Tel: 020-7928 7211
Fresh seafood served in imaginative ways in an informal, tiled restaurant behind Waterloo station. Second branch at *21 Wellington Street, WC2, tel: 020-7836 7161*. Moderate.

Sea Shell
49 Lisson Grove, NW1
Tel: 020-7723 8703
Renowned fish and chip restaurant and takeaway (carry-out). Although, as this traditional English delicacy goes, this restaurant is pricey, its wide choice of fish is very fresh and well cooked. Inexpensive.

Sheekey's
28–32 St Martin's Court, WC2
Tel: 020-7240 2565
Long-established restaurant, founded in the 1890s, close to the theatre district. Wide range of fish dishes, including several types of oyster in season. Moderate.

Upper Street Fish Shop
324 Upper Street, N1
Tel: 020-7359 1401
Friendly favourite in Islington. From basic cod and chips to oysters. Bring your own alcohol. Inexpensive.

Above: Livebait, near Southwark Station
Right: fashionable Kensington Place

French

Le Caprice
Arlington House, Arlington Street, SW1
Tel: 020-7629 2239
Brasserie-style restaurant, fashionable to graze and be seen in. Pianist in the evenings. Offers an excellent New York-style Sunday brunch. Moderate.

Club Gascon
57 West Smithfield, EC1
Tel: 020-7796 0600
Delicious earthy Gascon specialities such as *foie gras* prepared at least nine different ways. Dishes come in tapas-sized portions. Book as far in advance as possible. Moderate.

The Criterion
224 Piccadilly, W1
Tel: 020-7930 0488
The most affordable of chef Marco Pierre White's London restaurants. Modern French cuisine and a dining-room redolent of a Byzantine church. Moderate.

Manzi's
1–2 Leicester Street, WC2
Tel: 020-7734 0224
Timeless French restaurant serving traditional and well cooked fish dishes close to Leicester Square. Moderate.

Le Palais du Jardin
136 Long Acre, WC2
Tel: 020-7379 5353
Reliable brasserie food in civilised surroundings in Covent Garden. Moderate.

Saint M
St Martins Lane Hotel,
45 St Martin's Lane, WC2
Tel: 0800 634 5500
Classy rendition of a modern French brasserie in an outlandishly-designed hotel. Buzzing atmosphere, creative if small dishes, open 24 hours. Moderate.

Greek

Lemonia
89 Regents Park Road, NW1
Tel: 020-7586 7454
Probably London's best Greek restaurant – big, buzzing and friendly, and located in villagey Primrose Hill. Inexpensive.

Indian

Bombay Brasserie
Courtfield Close, SW7
Tel: 020-7370 4040
Excellent food and stylish decor that harks back to the days of the Raj. Try to get a table in the conservatory. Moderate–expensive.

Khan's
13 Westbourne Grove, W2
Tel: 020-7727 5420
Famous for its good value. Crowded in the evenings, the atmosphere is that of constant bustle. Don't expect to be able to linger too long over your meal. Inexpensive.

The Red Fort
77 Dean Street W1
Tel: 020-7437 2410
Respected and established Soho restaurant which offers superb Mogul cooking in comfortable surroundings. Moderate.

Italian

Bertorelli's
44A Floral Street, WC2
Tel: 020-7836 3969
Dependable and bustling Covent Garden restaurant with well-crafted regional dishes, as well as pastas and a good Italian wine list. Moderate.

Orso
27 Wellington Street, WC2
Tel: 020-7240 5269
Perennially popular with the theatre crowd. Pleasant ambience in spite of basement setting, with simple décor. Authentic northern Italian food. Moderate.

Pizza Express
10 Dean Street, W1
Tel: 020-7437 9595
Pizza Express is widely considered the best pizza chain in London. The Dean Street branch has the added attraction of live jazz in the basement. The classiest branch is **Pizza on The Park**, *11–13 Knightsbridge, tel: 020-7235 5273;* and the most fashionable one, complete with a separate champagne bar and a jazz pianist, is **Kettner's**, *29 Romilly Street, tel: 020-7287 8373*. No reservations necessary. Inexpensive.

Pollo
20 Old Compton Street, W1
Tel: 020-7734 5456
Dirt cheap, long-established Soho *trattoria*. No frills, but filling, down-to-earth portions of pasta. No reservations. Inexpensive.

Zafferano
15 Lowndes Street, SW1
Tel: 020-7235 5800
Zefferano is probably London's best Italian restaurant: first-class ingredients are turned into memorable dishes such as rabbit with Parma ham and polenta, and *grappa* ice-cream. Expensive.

Japanese

Wagamama
4 Streatham Street, WC1
Tel: 020-7323 9223
Good-value noodles, dumplings, etc. served at communal refectory tables. Enormously popular: expect a queue. Other branches at *10A Lexington Street* and *101A Wigmore Street*. No reservations. Inexpensive.

Malaysian

Melati
21 Great Windmill Street, W1
Tel: 020-7734 6964
In a rather seedy corner of Soho, Melati has been serving generous portions of flavoursome Malay/Indonesian cuisine for nearly two decades. Inexpensive.

Mexican

Café Pacifico
5 Langley Street, WC2
Tel: 020-7379 7728
Young, noisy Tex Mex joint in a converted Covent Garden warehouse. Inexpensive.

Pacific Rim

Sugar Club
21 Warwick Street, W1
Tel: 020-7437 7776
Exciting food concocted by Antipodean chefs influenced by Asian cuisines. Slick metropolitan setting. Moderate–expensive.

Russian

Borscht 'n' Tears
46 Beauchamp Place, SW3
Tel: 020-7589 5003
Zany Russian restaurant which attracts a young clientele. No reservations. Moderate.

Spanish

Moro
34–36 Exmouth Market, EC1
Tel: 020-7833 8336
Delicious Spanish/North African *tapas* and grills, a good choice of sherries, and a bubbly atmosphere. Informal. Moderate.

Thai

Churchill Arms
119 Kensington Church Street, W8
Tel: 020-7792 1246

Excellent Thai fare in the unlikely surroundings of a traditional-looking pub. Inexpensive.

Vegetarian

Mildred's
58 Greek Street, W1
Tel: 020-7494 1634
Imaginative cooking, well presented in café-style surroundings. Inexpensive.

Rasa
6 Dering Street, W1
Tel: 020-7629 1346
Accomplished vegetarian Keralan food in sophisticated surroundings. Non-smoking. Inexpensive–moderate.

Thai Garden
249 Globe Road, E2
Tel: 020-8981 5748
Award-winning vegetarian and seafood dishes. Inexpensive.

Places to be Seen

The Ivy
1 West Street, WC2
Tel: 020-7836 4751
High quality décor, gallery-worthy art, and good comfort food, such as beef braised in stout and spotted dick. Moderate.

Kensington Place
201 Kensington Church Street, W8
Tel: 020-7727 3184
Trendy and informal, this New York-style restaurant is always busy. Moderate.

Langan's Brasserie
Stratton Street, W1
Tel: 020-7491 8822
Langan's reputation for attracting celebrities often overshadows the food. Michael Caine is part owner. Moderate–expensive.

The Oxo Tower
Barge House Street, SE1
Tel: 020-7803 3888
On the top floor of the Oxo Tower Wharf building, an architecural landmark with river views. Brasserie and restaurant. Modern European food. Moderate–expensive.

Pharmacy
150 Notting Hill Gate, W11
Tel: 020-7221 2442
Celebrities, chemist's shop paraphernalia and cutting-edge art provide the backdrop for modern French/ English cuisine at this ultra-trendy restaurant and bar co-founded by artist Damien Hirst. Moderate–expensive.

Top Chefs

Chez Nico
90 Park Lane,W1
Tel: 020-7409 1290
A passionate perfectionist, Nico Ladenis serves classic French cuisine. If you dine here you can expect to enjoy a truly memorable meal. Very expensive (at least £100 per head for dinner).

Le Gavroche
43 Upper Brook Street, W1
Tel: 020-7408 0881
Formal, clubby atmosphere and imaginative French cuisine prepared by Michel Roux, son of the famous Albert. Very expensive (again, at least £100 per head for dinner).

Hotel Dining

Hotels such as **The Savoy**, **The Inn on the Park**, **The Connaught** and **The Capital** all have outstanding, formal restaurants. London's top hotels, such as **Claridges**, **The Ritz** and **The Savoy,** are also the best places for a traditional afternoon tea (scones, clotted cream, sandwiches, cakes), where it will cost the best part of £20 a head; book in advance. The **Waldorf Meridien** lays on tea dances at the weekend.

Above: Damien Hirst's post-modern, themed restaurant

BARS & PUBS

The following list is a selection of some the more characterful watering holes in the city.

Bars

The American Bar
Savoy Hotel, The Strand, WC2
Art deco timepiece. Jacket and tie required.

Atlantic Bar & Grill
20 Glasshouse Street, W1
Trendy, noisy haunt in a magnificent art deco ballroom done up to recreate the look of a 1930s cruise liner. Also a good restaurant.

Bar des Amis du Vin
11–13 Hanover Place, WC2
Dark, atmospheric basement bar with good wines and French snacks.

Market Bar
240A Portobello Road, W11
Exotically converted pub, now a fashionable Notting Hill hangout.

Pharmacy
150 Notting Hill Gate, W11
Trendy, fun, pharmaceutically-themed joke (the barstools are designed as aspirins).

Pubs

The Anchor
1 Bankside, SE1
Creaky and ancient, with a riverside terrace.

The Black Friar
174 Queen Victoria Street, EC4
Art Nouveau décor, located in the City.

Cutty Sark
Lassell Street, SE10
By the river in Greenwich; bags of character.

The Dove
19 Upper Mall, W6
Cosy old riverside inn in Hammersmith.

George Inn
77 Borough High Street, SE1
Lovely 17th-century coaching inn owned by the National Trust.

King's Head
115 Upper Street, N1
Islington pub with a theatre attached. Prices are quoted in the old pounds, shillings and pence.

Museum Tavern
49 Great Russell Street, WC1
Old-fashioned pub opposite the British Museum, where Karl Marx is said to have drunk.

The Spaniards Inn
Spaniards Lane, NW3
16th-century Hamsptead coaching inn with an attractive garden.

Ye Olde Cheshire Cheese
145 Fleet Street, EC4
Snug and historic 17th-century pub.

Above: the George Inn on the southern approach to London Bridge (see page 41)

NIGHTLIFE

Theatre

London's West End theatreland centres around Shaftesbury Avenue and Covent Garden, where some shows have been running for decades. Important venues beyond the West End include the **Royal National Theatre** on the South Bank, the **Royal Court** in Sloane Square, which has a reputation for groundbreaking work, and **The Donmar Warehouse** in Covent Garden and the **Almeida** in Islington, which have recently been enticing Hollywood celebrities to tread the boards.

West End shows are popular and tickets may be hard to obtain. If you can't book through the theatre box office (credit card bookings by telephone accepted) try Ticketmaster (020-7344 4000) and First Call (020-7420 0000) before going to other agencies who may charge a hefty fee. Avoid touts, as they will inevitably try to rip you off and sometimes have forged tickets.

The Half Price Ticket Booth on Leicester Square sells tickets for shows on the day of the performance only, at half price plus a small service charge. Only cash is accepted. The booth is open daily noon–6.30pm, except Sunday noon–3pm. Be prepared for long queues. Some theatres keep back a number of tickets for each performance to sell at the box office from 10am on the day.

Consult the listings in the weekly *Time Out* magazine, the *London Evening Standard* or quality national newspapers to find out what's on in the West End and the many fringe theatres around London.

Classical Music

The main venues are:

Barbican Centre
Silk Street, EC2
Tel: 020-7638 4141
Home to the London Symphony Orchestra.

Royal Albert Hall
Kensington Gore, SW7
Tel: 020-7589 8212
Hosts the popular 'Proms' every summer.

Royal Festival Hall
South Bank, SE1
Tel: 020-7960 4242
The most important classical music venue.

Wigmore Hall
36 Wigmore Street, W1
Tel: 020-7935 2141
Excellent for chamber concerts.

Ballet & Opera

The main venues are:

London Coliseum
St Martin's Lane, WC2
Tel: 020-7632 8300
Home to the English National Opera with performances from the Royal Festival Ballet and other major companies in the summer months.

The Royal Opera House
Covent Garden, WC2
Tel: 020-7304 4000
The home of the Royal Opera and Royal Ballet, reopened in 1999 after a controversial £214 million refit. Operas sung in their original language. Dressy.

Sadler's Wells
Rosebery Avenue, EC1
Tel: 020-7863 8000
Rebuilt in 1998; the top touring venue for first-rate British and international ballet and modern dance.

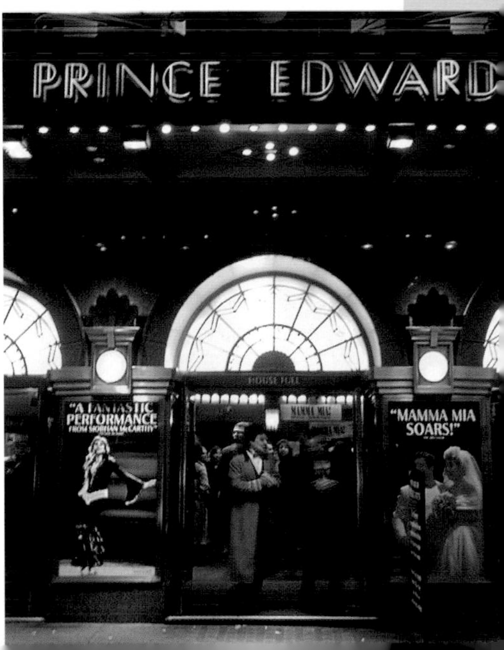

Right: Price Edward Theatre in the West End

Cinemas

Leicester Square is the place to catch newly-released films in cinemas fitted out with the latest technology. But be warned: tickets in the half a dozen multi-screen cinemas here are much more expensive than elsewhere (£8 or more in the evenings).

Institute of Contemporary Arts (ICA)
Nash House, The Mall, SW1
Tel: 020-7930 3647
Multi-arts centre with two cinemas showing experimental and foreign sub-titled films (*see page 27*).

National Film Theatre
South Bank, SE1
Tel: 020-7928 3232
High-brow films and classic revivals (*see page 38*).

Nightclubs

Many nightclubs feature 'one-nighters' which centre on a particular scene. Admission normally costs £5–15. Consult *Time Out* for full details, including the all-important dress code. Most places start hotting up between 11pm and midnight.

Equinox Discotheque
Leicester Square, WC2
Tel: 020-7437 1446
Huge, famous for its light show; this is one of the biggest discos in Europe, attracting a young crowd in smart casual dress.

The Fridge
Town Hall Parade, Brixton Hill, SW2
Tel: 020-7326 5100
Popular venue south of the river; renowned for spectacular one-nighters and gay-oriented nights.

Heaven
The Arches, Craven Street, WC2
Tel: 020-7930 2020
Beneath Charing Cross development is one of the best dance clubs in town. It's also the most famous gay club in London. Relaxed dress code.

Hippodrome
Charing Cross Road, WC2
Tel: 020-7437 4311
Incorporates all the technological tricks you could wish for. Smart but touristy.

Legends
29 Old Burlington Street, W1
Tel: 020-7437 9933
Glossy Mayfair club which attracts a fashionable, dressy crowd. Hosts a variety of one-nighters. Hip.

Limelight
136 Shaftesbury Avenue, W1
Tel: 020-7434 0572
A converted church; if you worship music, then the sound system will put you in touch with heaven.

Ministry of Sound
103 Gaunt Street, SE1
Tel: 020-7378 6528
This vast, impressive club has established itself as the top house music venue in London. Once you are in (expect long queues), you will be able to keep dancing well into the morning.

Salsa Club
96 Charing Cross Road, WC2
Tel: 020-7379 3277
A popular and friendly club/bar with an atmosphere which matches the exuberance of the Latin music played. Casual.

Left: advertising the National Film Theatre

Samantha's
2 New Burlington Street, W1
Tel: 020 7734 6249
Mainstream disco that has been around for a long time. Attracts well-dressed, mature clubbers. Smart.

Stringfellows
16 Upper St Martin's Lane, WC2
Tel: 020-7240 5534
No longer the fashionable venue it used to be, Stringfellows has acquired a somewhat tacky image.

Subterania
12 Acklam Road, Ladbroke Grove, W10
Tel: 020-8960 4590
Refreshingly well-designed modern interior, hewn out of the concrete of the Westway. Trendy.

Wag Club
35 Wardour Street, W1
Tel: 020-7437 5534
Soho club open until 6am at weekends. Heavy-duty dance music and fresh fruit bar to keep you going. Hip.

Comedy

The Comedy Store
1 Oxendon Street, W1
Tel: 020 7344 0234
Britain's best-known comedy venue, offering improvisation, open spots for masochists, and much more besides. Lots of famous performers – both on stage and in the audience.

Jongleurs Battersea
The Cornet, 49 Lavender Gardens, SW11
Tel: 020-7564 2500
A long-established venue featuring top stand-up comics. Other Jongleurs are situated in Camden and Bow in east London (same reservations number as above).

Cabaret

Madame Jo Jo's
8–10 Brewer Street, W1
Tel: 020-7734 2473
Lacking the sleaze and daring associated with Soho's past, Madame Jo Jo's still offers cabaret shows by leggy male lovelies (transvestites) in amazing glitzy costumes.

Jazz

Dover Street Wine Bar
8–9 Dover Street, W1
Tel: 020-7629 9813
Intimate basement where you can dine by candlelight whilst hearing live jazz, soul or R&B. Open till 3am. Popular with singles.

Jazz Café
5 Parkway, NW1
Tel: 020-7344 0044
Fantastic atmosphere in a modern, small-scale venue that hosts a very eclectic range of cutting-edge jazz groups.

100 Club
100 Oxford Street, W1
Tel: 020-7636 0933
Basic décor and two bars serving drinks at pub prices, this is a renowned venue for live jazz and rhythm-and-blues from established bands and young unknowns alike.

Ronnie Scott's
47 Frith Street, W1
Tel: 020-7439 0747
Ronnie Scott's is London's most famous jazz venue where the food and service come second to the music and the atmosphere. Arrive early, especially at weekends, as it remains popular despite the death in 1996 of its founder Ronnie Scott.

Above right: the start of a lads' night out

CALENDAR OF EVENTS

Specific dates for many of the following events vary from year to year. The London Tourist Board provides recorded information (*see page 90*), or consult *Time Out*.

January

London Parade (1st): celebratory parade from Parliament Square to Berkeley Square.
London International Boat Show, Earl's Court.
Charles I Commemoration (last Sunday): English Civil War Society dress up as Royalists and march from St James's Palace to Banqueting House.

February

Accession Day, opposite Dorchester Hotel, Hyde Park (6th): a 41-gun salute to mark the anniversary of the Queen's accession to the throne.
Chinese New Year: colourful Chinese celebrations with dragons and crafts, centring on Gerrard Street in Chinatown.
Great Spitalfields Pancake Day Race on Shrove Tuesday, 41 days before Easter or the day before Lent begins.

March

Ideal Home Exhibition, Earl's Court.
Oxford and Cambridge Boat Race: annual race between university oarsmen on the Thames between Putney and Mortlake.
Head of the Race: another boat race on the same route as above, but in the opposite direction from Mortlake to Putney, and this time with hundreds of crews.
Chelsea Antiques Fair, Old Town Hall, King's Road SW3.
London Harness Horse Parade, Battersea Park (Easter Monday): working horses draw carriages around the park.

April

London Marathon: one of the world's largest and most colourful, with many participants running for charity in fancy dress; route from Greenwich Park to Westminster.
Queen's Birthday (21st): the Queen's real birthday is celebrated with a gun salute in Hyde Park and at the Tower of London.

May

Chelsea Flower Show, Chelsea Royal Hospital: the world's most prestigious horticultural event, appealing to professionals and amateurs.
Royal Windsor Horse Show, Windsor Great Park.
FA Cup Final, Wembley: final of the nation's main football competition.
Oak Apple Day, Chelsea Royal Hospital: parade of Chelsea pensioners in memory of their founder, Charles II.

June

Beating the Retreat, Horse Guards Parade, Whitehall: ceremonial display of military bands.
Derby Day, Epsom Racecourse: famous flat horserace for three-year-old colts and fillies.
Royal Academy Summer Exhibition, Burlington House, Piccadilly: large exhibition of work by professional and amateur artists (until August).
Trooping the Colour, Horse Guards Parade (second Saturday): the Queen's 'official birthday' celebrations with a ceremonial parade of regimental colours, massed bands and a fly-past.
Royal Ascot: elegant and dressy race meeting attended by royalty.
Grosvenor House Art and Antiques Fair, Grosvenor House Hotel, Park Lane.
Wimbledon Lawn Tennis Championships: one of the year's sporting, and social, highlights.

Above: reveller at Notting Hill Carnival

City of London Festival: theatres, livery halls and churches in the City lay on highbrow musical entertainment (until mid-July).

July

Henley Royal Regatta, Henley on Thames, Oxfordshire: international rowing regatta. London society decamps to Oxfordshire for this important fixture in the social calendar.
Henry Wood Promenade Concerts, Royal Albert Hall: series of classical concerts known as 'The Proms'.
Swan Upping on the Thames: officials row up and down registering all the swans on the Thames.
Doggett's Coat and Badge Race, London Bridge: traditional race for single scull boats between London Bridge and Chelsea.
Greenwich and Docklands Festival: arts events at various venues north and south of the Thames.

August

Notting Hill Carnival, Ladbroke Grove (bank holiday weekend, end of month): colourful West Indian street carnival, the largest in Europe, with costumed parades, steel bands, stalls and huge crowds.

September

Horseman's Sunday, Church of St John and St Michael, W2: service dedicated to the horse, with mounted vicar and congregation.
The Great River Race: over 150 colourful craft, ranging from Viking-style longboats to Chinese dragonboats, race from Richmond to the Isle of Dogs.

October

Costermongers' Pearly Harvest Festival, Church of St Martin-in-the-Fields, Trafalgar Square (first Sunday): Pearly Kings and Queens from London's Cockney community attend this service in their traditional suits and frocks covered with pearl buttons.
Judges' Service: the British legal year begins with a procession of judges in full attire from Westminster Abbey to Parliament.
Horse of the Year Show, Wembley.
Trafalgar Day Parade (nearest Sunday to the 21st): commemorates Nelson's victory at Trafalgar.
London Motor Show, Earl's Court.

November

London to Brighton Veteran Car Run (first Sunday): hundreds of splendid veteran cars and their proud owners start out sedately from Hyde Park.
Lord Mayor's Show: grand procession from the Guildhall in the City to the Royal Courts of Justice, Aldwych, celebrating the Lord Mayor's election.
Guy Fawkes Night (5th): bonfires and firework displays in many of London's parks, marking Guy Fawkes's failure to blow up the Houses of Parliament in 1605. Especially good at Battersea Park and Parliament Hill.
Remembrance Sunday (nearest to the 11th): commemorates those lost at war, with the main wreath-laying service at the Cenotaph, Whitehall.
State Opening of Parliament, House of Lords, Westminster: the Queen officially reopens Parliament following the summer recess, preceded by a grand royal procession from Buckingham Palace to Westminster.
London Film Festival, National Film Theatre and West End cinemas: two weeks of international films.
Christmas Lights: switched on in Oxford and Regent streets.

December

International Showjumping Championships, Olympia Exhibition Centre.
January Sales: most start straight after Christmas, at the end of September.
New Year's Eve, Trafalgar Square: thousands congregate for a sometimes rowdy midnight celebration. (If you don't like crowds, you should go elsewhere.)

Right: a Pearly Queen at Costermongers' Festival in October

TELEPHONE
TELEPHONE
TELEPHONE
TEL
PULL

Practical *Information*

TRAVEL ESSENTIALS

Arriving by Air

From Heathrow Airport: The fastest way to reach central London is on the new high-speed train service, the Heathrow Express, to Paddington Station (tel: 0845 6001515). Trains leave 5.10am–11.40pm every 15 minutes and the journey takes 15–20 minutes. It's expensive at £12 one way. The cheapest way is via the Underground, on the Piccadilly line. It takes 50 minutes to Piccadilly Station and costs £3.50. By coach, take the red double-decker Airbus service. It picks up from all terminals, leaving at approximately half-hourly intervals between 5am and 10.30pm daily, and costs £7 one way. The A1 bus goes to Victoria, via Earl's Court and Knightsbridge, whilst the A2 bus goes to Russell Square, via Marble Arch and Baker Street. For 24-hour Airbus information, call 020 8400 6655. At non rush-hour times, the Airbus can be faster than the Underground. A black cab will cost upwards of £35 and can take over an hour depending on traffic.

From Gatwick Airport: Gatwick is served by mainline 'Gatwick Express' train services to Victoria Station. The train leaves every 15 minutes, except from 2–5am when it departs every 30 minutes. It takes just half an hour and costs £10.20 one way. Connex South Central's trains to Victoria take a few minutes longer but only cost £8.20, and operate around the clock. Jetlink 777 coaches (0990 747777) leave from both the North and South terminals and take about 90 minutes to reach Victoria. A single fare is £8.

From Luton Airport: A new direct train service to King's Cross was introduced at the end of 1999. The journey takes about 40 minutes. The Green Line 757 coach service to Victoria takes 75 minutes.

From Stansted Airport: There are trains every 15 or 30 minutes to Liverpool Street Station from 5am–11pm, Journey time is 45 minutes and tickets cost £11 one way.

From London City Airport: This airport is badly served by transport despite its close proximity to the city (6 miles/10km). The best option is the shuttle bus to Canary Wharf (10 minutes, costing £2) or Liverpool Street Station (25 minutes, £5), where you can pick up the main public transport network.

Eurostar

Eurostar trains (0990 186186) terminate at Waterloo International Station, on the south side of the river. Waterloo is well placed for Westminster, Covent Garden and the City. It is served by plenty of taxis, and the Northern, Bakerloo and Jubilee Underground lines.

Passports

Passport holders from most European countries, the Americas, South Africa, Japan and most Commonwealth countries do not generally require a visa to enter the UK for a short stay. If in any doubt check with the British Embassy in your home country before you leave.

Customs

Duty-free allowances for arrivees from non-European Union countries are as follows: 1

Left: one of the old-style call boxes.
Right: on an open-top tour bus

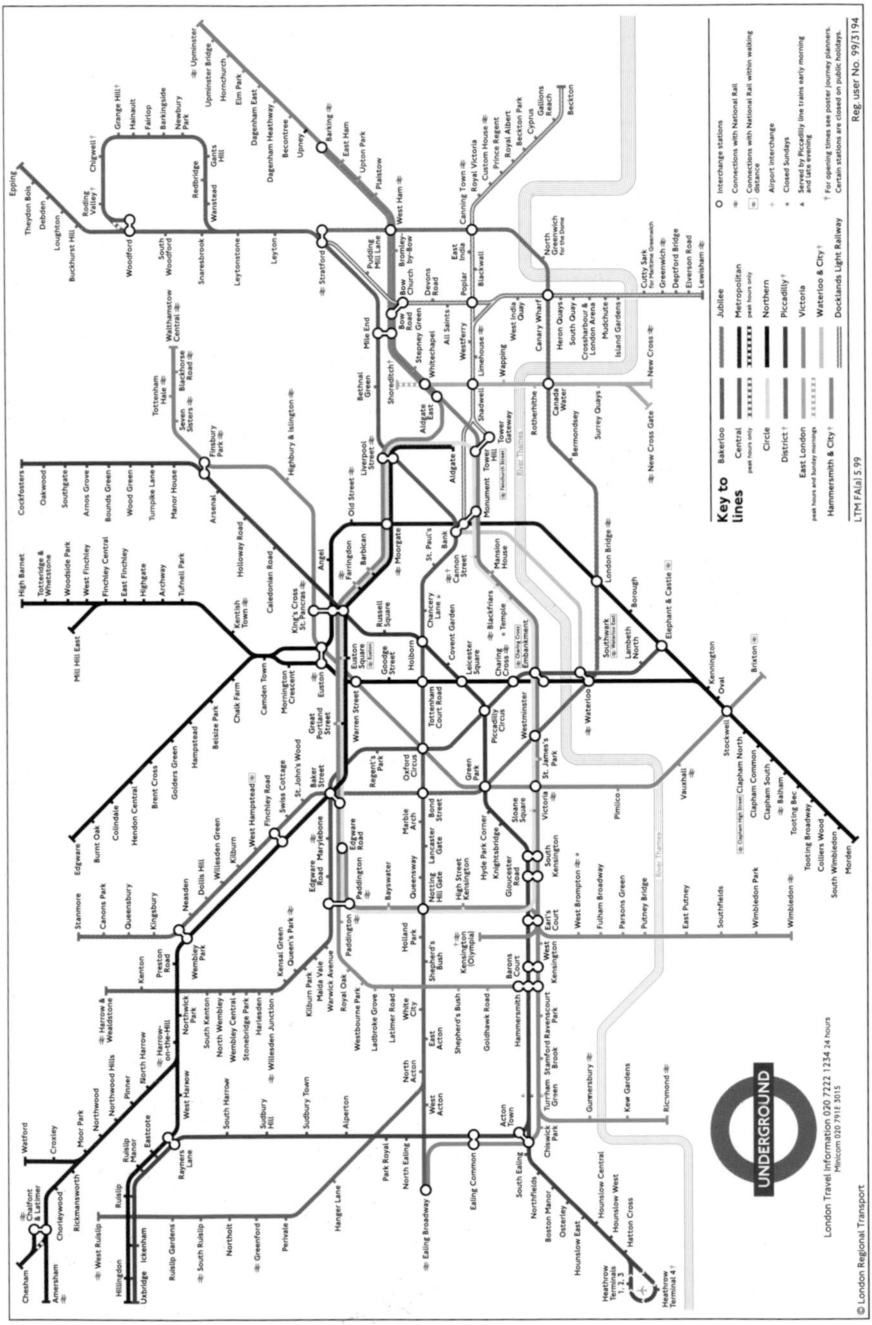
UNDERGROUND
Key to lines
Bakerloo
Central
peak hours only
Circle
District †
East London
peak hours and Sunday mornings
Hammersmith & City †
Jubilee
Metropolitan
peak hours only
Northern
Piccadilly †
Victoria
Waterloo & City †
Docklands Light Railway
Interchange stations
Connections with National Rail
Connections with National Rail within walking distance
Airport interchange
Closed Sundays
Served by Piccadilly line trains early morning and late evening
† For opening times see poster journey planners. Certain stations are closed on public holidays.
Reg. user No. 99/3194
LTM FA(a) 5.99
London Travel Information 020 7222 1234 24 hours
Minicom 020 7918 3015
London Regional Transport
River Thames

litre of spirits or 2 litres of fortified or sparkling wine and 2 litres of still table wine; 200 cigarettes or 100 cigarillos, or 50 cigars, or 250g of tobacco; 60cc perfume and 250cc toilet water; gifts or other goods up to a maximum value of £145. Duty free was abolished in 1999 for travel between EU countries, but EU visitors bringing goods on which duty has already been paid in their own countries have much more generous

quotas (such as 90 litres of wine and 800 cigarettes, or any amount likely to be for personal use).

It is prohibited to bring animals, plants, perishable foods, certain drugs, firearms and obscene material into the country without prior arrangement. There are no restrictions on the amount of foreign or British currency which can be brought into the UK.

Climate

London winters are cold and blustery, but snowfall is rare in the city. In high summer temperatures can reach above 80°F (27°C). But the weather is unpredictable and temperatures fluctuate considerably from day to day with surprise showers all year round. Come prepared with wet weather clothes and dress in layers. For recorded weather information, call 0839 500951 (peak rate).

Time

British Summer Time (BST) begins in March when the nation puts its clocks forward one hour, and ends in October when clocks go back to Greenwich Mean Time (GMT).

Above: railwayman at the ready
Right: a familiar beacon

Public Holidays

New Year's Day, Good Friday, Easter Monday, May Day (first Monday in May), Spring Bank Holiday (last Monday in May), August Bank Holiday (last Monday in August), Christmas Day, Boxing Day (26 December). Many shops now stay open on most bank holidays, as public holidays are called in the UK.

Electricity

The electrical current in the UK is 220–240 volts. Most hotels have 110-volt shaving sockets.

Business Hours

Shopping hours in London are usually 9am–5.30pm Monday to Saturday. Shops in the centre of town rarely close for lunch and may stay open later, particularly around Covent Garden and Piccadilly Circus. Some shops are open on Sunday (especially newsagents, small grocery shops and large warehouse stores away from the centre). Late-night shopping, until as late as 8pm, is on Thursday in Oxford and Regent streets and on Wednesday in Knightsbridge and Kensington.

GETTING AROUND

Public Transport

The ageing Underground (also known as the Tube) is the quickest way to get around. It runs from around 5.30am until shortly after midnight, and is extremely busy in the rush hours (8–9.30am and 5–6.30pm). Ensure you have a valid ticket and keep hold of it after you have passed through the electronic barriers as it is illegal to travel without one. Fares are based on a zone system.

Smoking is prohibited. The latest development of the network is an extension to the Jubilee line, connecting Waterloo with Canary Wharf and North Greenwich (the station for the Millennium Dome).

The Docklands Light Railway, which opened in 1987, is an excellent way to see the modern re-development of London's old dock area. A fully automated system, it has two branches running from Bank and - Stratford to Island Gardens (on the Isle of Dogs) and Beckton, plus an extension linking the Isle of Dogs to Greenwich and Lewisham, which opened in 1999. The service is organised in the same way as the Tube.

London buses provide a comprehensive service throughout Greater London and have their route and number clearly displayed on the front. On most buses, you pay the driver, but on the old Routemasters where you board at the rear, a conductor will come and collect your fare. Unlike the Underground, buses carry on running on certain routes hourly throughout the night, radiating from Trafalgar Square (these buses are prefixed 'N' for night).

Tickets and Travelcards

The One Day Travelcard is a day pass that allows unlimited travel within London on the Tube, buses, Docklands Light Railway and national railways for £3.90–4.70 (depending on how many zones you are travelling through). The Travelcard can be used after 9.30am on weekdays and all day Saturday, Sunday and public holidays. It is readily available from all Underground and railway stations.There are also weekend and family Travelcards. Travelcards for a week (£15.30–35.40) or a month's travel (£58.80–136), for which you require a passport-sized photograph, can be used at any time. You can also save money travelling in zone 1 (central London) by purchasing a Carnet of 10 tickets for £11.

Take care not to travel without a ticket or with the wrong ticket – if caught, you will automatically be fined £10, regardless of your excuse.

Taxis

London's famous black cabs are licensed and display the strictly regulated charges on a meter. Their drivers are well trained, having had to complete a rigorous study of the capital's streets (acquiring 'The Knowledge') before being able to take to the road. You can hail a cab or phone for one on 020-7272 0272.

Minicabs are not allowed to compete with black cabs on the streets and must be summoned by telephone or from a minicab kiosk. Though cheaper than black cabs, they are less reliable. Make sure you agree upon a fee before setting off and, unlike in black cabs, don't expect them to know precise destinations.

On the River

Boat trips are an excellent way to see many of London's sights. The Westminster Passen-

Above: Thames riverboats combine transport and sightseeing

ger Service Association (tel: 020-7930 2062) runs a riverboat service from Westminster Pier upriver to Kew, Richmond and Hampton Court from Easter to October. Cruises down-river to the Tower of London, St Katharine's Dock, Greenwich and the Thames Barrier run year round: contact Crown River Cruises (tel: 020-7936 2033), Thames Cruises (tel: 020-7930 3373) or Catamaran Cruises (020-7987 1185). White Horse Fast Ferries (tel: 01474 566220) operates a ferry service 6.30am–8.30pm weekdays, and a more limited service at weekends, between Canary Wharf and the South Bank, with several stops on the way: £1.90 a ticket. City Cruises (tel: 020-7488 0344) runs a ferry service between Westminster and the Tower every 30 minutes throughout the year (£4.60 single, £5.80 return, children half-price); during 2000 the company is also running a river service to the Millennium Dome from under the London Eye at Waterloo pier and from Blackfriars pier every 30 minutes from 9.30am (£8.40 adults return, children £5.20 return).

For a full timetable of services, contact London Travel Information on 020-7222 1234, and ask for the Thames River Services booklet.

Driving

In the UK, drive on the left and observe the speed limits: 30mph (50kph) in urban areas, 60mph (96kph) on A roads away from built-up areas, and 70mph (112kph) on motorways and dual carriageways. It is illegal to drink and drive, and penalties are severe. The law also states that drivers and passengers must wear seat-belts where available. Cars should give way to pedestrians at zebra crossings.

Driving in London, with its maze of one-way streets, impatient drivers, congestion and parking problems, can be a nightmare, and is definitely not recommended to anyone unfamiliar with the city. Parking is extremely difficult in central London. Meters are slightly cheaper than car parks, but only allow parking for a maximum of two hours. If using a meter, don't leave your car parked a moment longer than your time allows and do not return and insert more money once your time has run out. These are offences for which you can face a fine in the region of £30 and there are plenty of traffic wardens ready to give out tickets. Meter parking is free in most parts of central London after 6.30pm Monday to Friday and all day Sunday; regulations on Saturday vary. Always check the details given on the meter so as not to be caught out.

Don't ever leave your car on a double yellow line or in areas reserved for residents and permit holders, as you are liable to have your wheels clamped or your car towed away, and face an exceptionally heavy fine as well as considerable inconvenience to reclaim your vehicle.

Car Rental

To rent a car in Britain you should be over 21 years old and have held a valid full driving licence for more than one year.

The cost of hiring a car will usually include insurance and unlimited mileage. It does not, however, include insurance cover for accidental damage to interior trim, wheels and tyres or insurance for other drivers without prior approval. It can be worth shopping around before deciding on a car, as some companies offer special weekend and holiday rates.

If you intend to combine a visit to the rest of the UK with a stay in London, it is best to concentrate on London first and then hire a car when you leave the city.

Car Rental Companies

Avis: 0990 900500.
Budget: 0800 181181.
Europcar: 0345 222525.
Hertz Rent-a-car: 0990 906090.
Holiday Autos: 0990 300400.

24-hour Car Parks

There are a number of 24-hour NCP car parks in central London – call 020-740 43777. Useful ones in the West End can be found at Brewer Street, Upper St Martin's Lane and Wardour Street. Rates vary, but are invariably expensive – from £7–13 for 3 hours.

24-hour Breakdown Assistance

AA: 0800 887766.
RAC: 0800 828282.
Green Flag Emergency Assistance: 0800 400600.

Above: this way to the South Bank Centre

TOURIST INFORMATION

London's official tourism organisation is the London Tourist Board (LTB). At the following tourist information centres the LTB provides general information and booking services for hotels, theatre and sightseeing tours: Heathrow terminals 1, 2 and 3 (Underground station concourse, daily 8am– 6pm, and Terminal 3 Arrivals concourse, daily 6am–11pm), Waterloo International Arrivals Hall (daily 8.30am–10.30pm), Victoria Station (summer: daily 8am–7pm; winter: Mon–Sat 8am–6pm, Sun 8.30am–4pm) and Liverpool Street Station (Mon–Fri 8am–6pm, weekends 8.45am–5.30pm).

Only local visitor centres – such as Greenwich (tel: 020-8858 6376) and Southwark (tel: 020-7403 8299) – handle telephone enquiries; you must visit the city centre offices in person. The LTB also provides limited recorded information on 020-7932 2000. It also offers a more extensive recorded information service, covering various subjects including forthcoming events, on a series of peak rate numbers; tel: 020-7971 0026 for details. The LTB's web site is www.LondonTown.com.

Travel Information Centres provide maps, timetables and advice at the following Underground stations: Victoria, Piccadilly Circus, Oxford Circus, Euston, Liverpool Street, King's Cross and St James's Park.

The Britain Visitor Centre at No 1 Regent Street provides comprehensive travel, accommodation, entertainment and sightseeing information and booking services for the whole of Britain. Open Mon 9.30am–6.30pm, Tues–Fri 9am–6.30pm, weekends 10am–4pm.

More Information by Phone

London Travel Information (24 hours): 020-7222 1234.

Artsline, arts information for the disabled: 020-7388 2227.

National Trust: 020-7222 9251.

Special events for children: 0839 123404.

MONEY MATTERS

Banks are open 9.30am–4/4.30pm Mon–Fr, and some also open on Saturday morning. The major banks (Lloyds, Barclays, HSBC and National Westminster) can be found on most high streets and tend to offer similar exchange rates. They charge no commission on travellers' cheques presented in sterling or for changing a cheque in another currency if the bank is connected to your own bank at home. However, there will be a charge for changing cash into another currency or for giving cash against a credit card. There are automatic tellers outside most banks where appropriate credit or cashpoint cards can be used to obtain cash.

Money may also be changed by travel agents, such as Thomas Cook, and at some large department stores. There are also numerous Bureaux de Change throughout London, but you should be wary of changing money at these as they may rip you off. If you do have to use one, try to ensure it's carrying the LTB code of conduct sticker. Chequepoint is a reputable chain with 24-hour branches at Piccadilly Circus, Marble Arch, Earl's Court and Bayswater Underground stations.

Credit cards are widely accepted in shops, hotels and restaurants in London, although you should watch out for the few exceptions. Eurocheques are becoming more acceptable.

Tipping

Good service in restaurants and hotels and from cab drivers, hairdressers, porters and sightseeing guides should be rewarded with a tip of not less than 10 per cent. Tipping any other service has to be gauged carefully as in some cases it may offend. It is not customary to tip in bars and pubs, theatres and cinemas. Restaurants may automatically add a 10–15 percent service charge to your bill, which should be specified on the tariff (make sure you don't pay twice for service, especially if paying by credit card where the total box may be left open). If you have justifiable reason to be dissatisfied, you may deduct the service charge.

COMMUNICATION

Telephone

British Telecom provides both public coin call boxes and booths that accept only phone cards (resembling credit cards and widely available from post offices and newsagents for varying amounts), or credit cards.

Tthe dialling code for London is 020, followed by an eight-figure number. Old seven-figure numbers should be prefixed with a 7 for inner London numbers and by 8 for outer London numbers.

International Calls

To dial other countries, first dial the international access code 00, then the country code: Australia (61); France (33); Germany (49); Italy (39); Japan (81); Netherlands (31); Spain (34); US and Canada (1). If using a US credit phone card, dial the company's access number – Sprint: 0800 89 0877; AT&T: 0800 89 0011; Worldphone: 0800 89 0222.

Cyber Cafés

These are proliferating and most make it easy to send e-mails. A few convenient locations are: Cyberia, 39 Whitfield Street, W1 (near Goodge Street Tube station); Café Internet, 22–24 Buckingham Palace Road, SW1 (near Victoria Station); and Cyberspy, 15 Golden Square, W1 (near Tottenham Court Road Tbse station.

Useful Numbers

Emergencies (for police, fire and ambulance): 999
Operator (for technical difficulties with UK numbers): 100
Directory Enquiries (UK): 192
International Operator: 155
International Directory Enquiries: 153
Speaking Clock: 123

Postal Services

Most post offices are open Mon–Fri 9am–5.30pm, Sat 9am–noon. Stamps are available from post offices, or from vending machines outside, and from some newsagents and shops. It costs 26p to send a letter first class in the UK, 20p for second class. To send a postcard to an EU destination costs 34p, and 37p worldwide.

London's main post office is on Trafalgar Square, situated on the east side near the church of St Martin-in-the-Fields, and is open Mon–Fri 8am–8pm, Sat 9am–8pm. There are plenty of other local offices.

HEALTH & EMERGENCIES

In an absolute emergency call 999 for fire, ambulance or police. Otherwise, call Directory Enquiries on 192 and ask for the number of the nearest police station or hospital casualty department, or your country's embassy in London.

Unless you come from an EU country or your country has reciprocal arrangements with the UK, you will be liable for the cost of medical treatment and should therefore have adequate health insurance before you arrive.

In medical and dental emergencies:
Great Chapel Street Medical Centre, 13 Great Chapel Street W1 (020-7437 9360), is a National Health Service clinic with afternoon surgery Monday to Friday, where anyone can walk in off the street without an appointment and be treated.

Right: for home thoughts

Emergency dental care: Call Eastman's Dental Hospital on 020-7915 1000.

Chemists: Boots is Britain's largest chain of pharmacies, with numerous branches throughout London which will make up prescriptions while you wait. The branch at 114 Queensway W2 is open until 10pm daily, whilst Bliss Chemist at Marble Arch is open until midnight daily.

LOST PROPERTY

For possessions lost on buses or the Tube, contact London Transport Lost Property Office, 200 Baker Street NW1 (tel: 020-7486 2496), 9.30am–2pm Mon–Fri. The Taxi Lost Property Office (black cabs only) is at 15 Penton Street N1 (tel: 020-7833 0996), open 9am–4pm Mon–Fri.

LEFT LUGGAGE

Most main railway stations have left luggage departments where you can leave your suitcases on a short-term basis, and/or provide lockers in which items can be left for 24 hours. These offices open around 7am and close at around 10–11pm.

MEDIA

Newspapers and Magazines

The quality national daily newspapers are *The Times* and the *Daily Telegraph* (right bias), *The Guardian* (centre-left bias) and *The Independent* (centre). There are also the *Financial Times* and the weekly *European*. Tabloids such as *The Sun*, *The Star* and *The Mirror* are smaller with news issues swamped by pages of gossip. Mid-market papers are the *Daily Mail* and *Daily Express*. Most papers have a Sunday edition with a colour supplement.

For information listings on entertainment and events in London, consult the weekly magazine *Time Out*, published every Wednesday. London's local paper is the *Evening Standard* which comes out on weekday lunchtimes. Although it covers major international news, it is mainly concerned with events and information relating to the capital, and also contains extensive classified advertisements. Foreign newspapers and magazines are available from the following newsagents:

Capital Newsagents, 48 Old Compton Street, W1

Moroni's of Soho, 68 Old Compton Street, W1

Selfridges, Oxford Street, W1

W H Smiths: most large city centre branches and outlets at many railway stations.

Television

Britain has five major television channels: BBC1, BBC2, ITV and channels 4 and 5. They have a reputation for broadcasting some of the best-quality television in the world. However, with the advent of satellite television and independent television franchising, changes are taking place as stations become more commercially motivated and biased towards mass audience programmes such as soap operas, game shows and sit-coms. The two British Broadcasting Corporation channels (BBC1 and BBC2) do not rely on advertising for financial support, whereas the other, independent channels are funded by advertising. BBC2 broadcasts more cultural and serious programmes than BBC1 whilst Channel 4 is less mainstream and more pioneering than ITV, commissioning films and broadcasting programmes of specialist interest. Recent years have seen an epidemic of satellite dishes appearing on houses in the UK, providing TV addicts with 24-hour news, music, films and sporting events. Cable television is a popular alternative to satellite, with more channels to choose from, and digital television is just taking off.

Radio

Many new, independent stations have sprung up in recent years. However, the BBC continues to dominate the British airwaves with:

Radio 1, 98.8FM, mainly pop

Radio 2, 89.1FM, easy-listening

Radio 3, 91.3FM, classical music

Radio 4, 93.5FM, news, current affairs, consumer affairs and drama

Radio 5, 909MW, general interest, news and sport

GLR (Greater London Radio), 94.9FM, music, chat and current affairs

London's most popular independent stations:
Capital fm, 95.8FM, 24-hour pop
Capital Gold, 1548MW, 24-hour golden oldies
London Newstalk 1152MW, news, discussion and phone-ins
Jazz fm, 102.2FM, 24-hour jazz
Kiss fm, 100FM, 24-hour dance

ACCOMMODATION

London hotel prices are higher than in any other major city in Europe – and you don't necessarily get much for your money. Some budget accommodation is simply appalling, and many more expensive hotels are dull and unmemorable.

The accommodation listed below (almost all in central London) is the best the city has to offer to suit all pockets – from simple bed-and-breakfasts (B&Bs) to the new crop of ultra-trendy, minimalist-designed hotels. Grande dames such as the Ritz are included too, as are small luxury 'town house' pads, which have fewer facilities but are cosier and offer a more personal service. Most luxury hotels are in Mayfair, while the best hunting grounds for relatively cheap B&B accommodation are Victoria, Earl's Court, Bayswater and Bloomsbury.

In the peak seasons (Chistmas, Easter and April to September), book well in advance. The London Tourist Board provides an accommodation booking service through its information centres or by phone (credit or debit cards only): tel: 020-7604 2890. At less busy times of the year, many hotels offer discounted weekend rates. It's also worth bargaining with large hotels, especially if you're booking at short notice.

B&Bs offer an alternative to impersonal hotels, where you stay as a paying guest in a private home. The London Bed & Breakfast Agency (tel: 020-7586 2768) has some 200 homes on its books, with prices from around £40–80 for a double room per night. Uptown Reservations (tel: 020-7351 3445) has a smaller, more upmarket selection: double rooms with private bath cost £85.

London has seven youth hostels run by the Youth Hostel Association. Beds in dormitories cost from around £16–22 per night. Call the YHA on 01727-855215 for more details. A good independent hostel is the Generator (tel: 020-7388 7666), in a funky, futuristic block on Compton Place in Bloomsbury. Its prices are normally higher than in YHAs, since you don't share with strangers.

The price bands below are for two people sharing the cheapest double room, including tax (VAT at 17.5 percent) and breakfast. Note that B&Bs normally include VAT and breakfast in their quoted rates, whereas upmarket hotels don't. Together, they can add as much as £60–90 on to a single night's stay.

Luxury (over £250)

The Berkeley
Wilton Place, SW1
Tel: 020-7235 6000
Fax: 020-7235 4330
Deluxe, refined Knightsbridge hotel which is considered to be one of Britain's finest. Period detailing has been transported from the old Berkeley, which was in Piccadilly before moving here in 1972. Rooms are comfortably furnished in a traditional English style, some with terraces. There is a Roman bath-style rooftop pool, gymnasium and sauna. 168 rooms.

The Capital
Basil Street, SW3
Tel: 020-7589 5171
Fax: 020-7225 0011
E-mail: reservations@capitalhotel.co.uk
Intimate town house in the heart of Knightsbridge. Relaxed and comfortable with courteous service and *fin de siècle* elegance. The restaurant has one Michelin star and serves fine French cuisine. The 48 rooms are tastefully furnished.

Right: luxury treatment

Above: Blakes Hotel has a showbiz clientele

The Connaught
Carlos Place, W1
Tel: 020-7499 7070
Fax: 020-7495 3262
E-mail: info@the-connaught.co.uk
A peerless, luxury Mayfair bastion that offers the best of old-fashioned English hospitality – namely faultless service, a clubby formal restaurant and 90 elegant bedrooms.

Hempel
31–35 Craven Hill Gardens, W2
Tel: 020-7298 9000
Fax: 020-7402 4666
E-mail: the-hempel@easynet.co.uk
This Bayswater temple to oriental minimalism is as extraordinary looking as hotels get. Though an aesthetic *tour de force*, the 46 rooms are so weirdly designed that it can be hard to find the loo.

The Metropolitan
19 Old Park Lane, W1
Tel: 020-7447 1047
Fax: 020-7447 1100
E-mail: res@metropolitan.co.uk
An achingly trendy new Mayfair hotel, with supermodels for clientele and staff in the slickest designer gear. A highly-rated Japanese restaurant, an exclusive bar for members and hotel residents only, and 155 stark, minimalist bedrooms.

One Aldwych
1 Aldwych, WC2
Tel: 020-7300 1000
Fax: 020-7300 1001
E-mail: sales@onealdwych.co.uk
One of the most restrained of the crop of London's new, individual hotels, housed in an Edwardian bank. Excellent, sophisticated restaurants, a swimming pool with underwater music, and fabulous bathrooms with black marble baths and TVs. 105 rooms.

The Ritz
Piccadilly, W1
Tel: 020-7493 8181
Fax: 020-7493 2687
E-mail: inquire@theritzhotel.co.uk
Timeless hotel with overtones of sheer decadence; synonymous with class and style the world over. Even if you don't stay here, it is worth coming for breakfast or tea. 131 rooms.

The Savoy
The Strand, WC2
Tel: 020-7836 4343
Fax: 020-7240 6040
E-mail: info@the-savoy.co.uk
Arguably the most atmospheric of London's landmark hotels. Famous for its teas, its formal Grill Room restaurant, and top-notch service. The 207 bedrooms – the most individual in Art Deco style – all have wonderful marble bathrooms.

Expensive (£170–250)

The Basil Street Hotel
Basil Street, SW3
Tel: 020-7581 3311
Fax: 020-7581 3693
E-mail: thebasil@aol.com
Old-fashioned Knightsbridge hotel with plenty of English charm. Built in 1910, it is privately owned and attracts a regular clientele of tweedy types up from the country. Rooms are traditional and comfortable. Ladies-only club. 95 rooms.

The Beaufort
33 Beaufort Gardens, SW3
Tel: 020-7584 5252
Fax: 020-7589 2834
Excellent small town-house hotel in an elegant Knightsbridge square, which works hard to maintain its fine reputation. Guests are given a front door key and invited to help themselves to drinks and food (room service menu) and have use of a nearby health club, all included in the room price. The pastel rooms are filled with extras such as a decanter of brandy, Swiss chocolates, fruit, flowers and even an umbrella. 28 rooms.

Blakes
33 Roland Gardens, SW7
Tel: 020-7370 6701
Fax: 020-7373 0442
E-mail: blakes@easynet.co.uk
Notable for its alternative style, this exotic, laid-back hotel is popular with those in the entertainment industries. It is the creation of actress and interior designer Anouska Hempel. 52 rooms.

The Cadogan
75 Sloane Street, SW1
Tel: 020-7235 7141
Fax: 020-7245 0994
E-mail: info@thecadogan.u-net.com
This fine Edwardian building was once home to actress and society beauty, Lillie Langtry, and it has associations with Oscar Wilde. Old-fashioned elegance has been combined with modern comforts. 62 rooms.

Cannizaro House
West Side, Wimbledon Common, SW19
Tel: 020-8879 1464
Fax: 020-8879 7338
A grand 18th-century country house hotel on the edge of Wimbledon Common, in as rural a setting as London can offer. The more interesting of the 46 bedrooms lie in the original building.

The Gore
189 Queen's Gate, SW7
Tel: 020-7584 6601
Fax: 020-7589 8127
E-mail: sales@gorehotel.co.uk
An idiosyncratic Kensington hotel occupying two Victorian mansions close to the Royal Albert Hall. Every inch of wall space is covered in paintings and prints. Slick bistro and buzzing bar, and 54 individual bedrooms.

The Goring
15 Beeston Place, SW1
Tel: 020-7396 9000
Fax: 020-7834 4393
E-mail: reception@goringhotel.co.uk
Just behind Buckingham Palace is this gracious hotel, run by the Goring family since 1910 when it was the first hotel in the world to have a bathroom and central heating in every room. 75 rooms decorated in a dignified fashion.

Hazlitt's
6 Frith Street, W1
Tel: 020-7434 1771
Fax: 020-7439 1524
E-mail: reservations@hazlitts.co.uk
A 'classy B&B', popular with media and literary types, occupying three historic 18th-century town houses in Soho. The 23 rooms are charmingly furnished in classic period style with antiques, plants, and Victorian bath fittings.

L'Hotel
28 Basil Street, SW3
Tel: 020-7589 6286
Fax: 020-7823 7826
E-mail: lhotel@capitalgrp.co.uk
Sister to, and next-door-but-one from, the grand Capital (see Luxury category), this upmarket B&B is beautifully decorated in French country style. 12 rooms and few facilities other than a slick modern wine bar/bistro in the basement.

myhotel bloomsbury
11–13 Bayley Street, WC1
Tel: 020-7667 6000
Fax: 020-7667 6001
E-mail: guest_services@myhotels.co.uk
A spare elegance characterises this new hotel created by the Conran Design Partnership along Feng Shui lines. Tranquillity is assured, and guests are allocated a personal assistant for their stay. 76 rooms.

Left: old-fashioned elegance at The Cadogan

St Martin's Lane
45 St Martin's Lane, WC2
Tel: 020-7300 5500
Fax: 020-7300 5501
Presently the hippest hotel in London, created by American entrepreneur Ian Schrager and French designer Philippe Starck. Outlandish lighting, crazy furniture, good expensive food, and 204 fun, blindingly white bedrooms.

Tower Thistle Hotel
St Katharine's Way, E1
Tel: 020-7481 2575
Fax: 020-7481 3799
What this large modern hotel lacks in charm is compensated for by its location on the bank of the Thames, surrounded by the Tower of London, Tower Bridge and St Katharine's Dock. It is a handy choice for businessmen who want to be near the City. 801 rooms.

Moderate (£90–170)

Abbey Court
20 Pembridge Gardens, W2
Tel: 020-7221 7518
Fax: 020-7792 0858
E-mail: abbeyhotel@aol.com
A beautifully-restored Notting Hill town house where great attention is paid to detail. Rooms are furnished in English country style, all with Italian marble bathrooms with whirlpool baths. 22 rooms.

Academy Hotel
17–25 Gower Street, WC1
Tel: 020-7631 4115
Fax: 020-7636 3442
E-mail: resacademy@etontownhouse.com
Occupying five nicely converted Georgian town houses in the heart of literary Bloomsbury. The dining room is 1980s design; the 48 rooms are more traditionally furnished. Quieter ones overlook a small walled garden to the rear.

Durrants Hotel
George Street, W1
Tel: 020-7935 8131
Fax: 020-7487 3510
Located just north of Oxford Street; discreet family-run hotel with the old-fashioned atmosphere of a country inn. Public rooms furnished with old wood panelling. Bedrooms recently renovated in feminine styles. Well priced for the area. 97 rooms.

Five Sumner Place
5 Sumner Place, SW7
Tel: 020-7584 7586
Fax: 020 -823 9962
E-mail: reservations@sumnerplace.com
Civilised South Kensington B&B on a smart Victorian terrace: pretty conservatory breakfast room and 11 well-equipped bedrooms.

Knightsbridge Green Hotel
159 Knightsbridge, SW1
Tel: 020-7584 6274
Fax: 020-7225 1635
E-mail: thekghotel@aol.com
A town house B&B hidden away between, and yards from, Harrods and Hyde Park. The 27 spruce, contemporary-styled bedrooms are very good value for the location.

Miller's
111A Westbourne Grove, W2
Tel: 020-7243 1024
Fax: 020-7243 1064
E-mail: enquiries@millersuk.com
An idiosyncratic B&B owned by a well-known antique collector that feels more like a fascinating antiques' shop than a hotel. The 7 plush bedrooms are themed after Romantic poets.

Number Sixteen
16 Sumner Place, SW7
Tel: 020-7589 5232
Fax: 020-7584 8615.
E-mail: reservations@numbersixteenhotel.co.uk
Four interconnected terraced houses on a quiet South Kensington side street, turned into a B&B with the air of a refined but relaxing country house. 36 rooms.

Portobello Hotel
22 Stanley Gardens, W11
Tel: 020-7727 2777
Fax: 020-7792 9641
Somewhat eccentric, furnished in a hybrid Victorian/Moroccan/oriental style, this trendy Notting Hill hotel is close to Portobello's antique market. The 24 rooms vary from tiny cabins to unusual four-poster suites.

The Rubens
Buckingham Palace Road, Victoria, SW1
Tel: 020-7834 6600
Fax: 020-7828 5401
Ideally situated opposite the Royal Mews, close to Buckingham Palace, this smartly modernised hotel is decorated in pretty pastel shades with elegant furniture. The Rubens provides a high, traditional standard of service. 174 rooms.

Tophams Belgravia
28 Ebury Street, SW1
Tel: 020-7730 8147
Fax: 020-7823 5966.
E-mail:tophams_belgravia@compuserve.com
This characterful, family-run hotel, spread over five interconnected terraced houses on a busy street in Victoria, has a warren of passages and lots of cute little rooms. An old-fashioned atmosphere, and faithful clientele. 39 rooms.

Wilbraham Hotel
71–75 Wilbraham Place, SW1
Tel: 020-7730 8296
Fax: 020-7730 6815
This privately-owned, old-fashioned hotel has a distinct English charm and offers good value in exclusive Belgravia. Meals are served in the panelled Butlery Bar. The 47 bedrooms are well kept but they have few fancy frills.

The Willett
32 Sloane Gardens, SW1
Tel: 020-7824 8415
Fax: 020-7730 4830
An excellent, good value small hotel in a fashionable neighbourhood – it's on a quiet Victorian terrace yards from Sloane Square. The hotel has been modernised in a tasteful light and airy style. 19 rooms.

Budget (under £90)

Abbey House
11 Vicarage Gate, W8
Tel: 020-7727 2594
A grand Victorian house on a desirable Kensington side street. Though furnished in a basic manner, it is well maintained and spruced up annually. 15 rooms (none en suite). No credit cards.

County Hall Travel Inn
Belvedere Road, SE1
Tel. 020-7902 1600
Fax: 020-7902 1619
Large budget chain hotel occupying part of the former County Hall building (*see page 41*) by the Thames. Rates for the 313 rooms are as good value as any in London, given their spaciousness and the hotel's prime, central location.

Edward Lear Hotel
28–30 Seymour Street, W1
Tel: 020-7402 5401
Fax: 020-7706 3766
E-mail: edwardlear@aol.com
This Georgian house close to Marble Arch was once home to the Victorian painter and poet Edward Lear. The 31 bedrooms are comfortable and modern.

Elizabeth Hotel
37 Eccleston Square, SW1
Tel: 020-7828 6812
Fax: 020-7828 6814
This is a small private hotel overlooking a period square in Pimlico, close to Victoria. Residents have use of private gardens and a tennis court. 37 small rooms, most en suite.

Above:

Hampstead Village Guesthouse
2 Kemplay Road, NW3
Tel: 020-7435 8679
Fax: 020-7794 0254
E-mail: hvguesthouse@dial.pipex.com
Late Victorian house near the centre of Hampstead run informally as a B&B. The bedrooms are full of family clobber and interesting antiques, and feel like spare rooms in a friend's home. Breakfast is served in the kitchen or the courtyard garden. 6 rooms (most en suite).

Windermere
142–144 Warwick Way, SW1
Tel: 020-7834 5163
Fax: 020-7630 8831
E-mail: windermere@compuserve.com
One of the best of the many budget hotels near Victoria station, with a fresh-looking little sitting-room and basement restaurant, and 22 cheerful bedrooms. Some traffic noise, but double-glazing.

Woodville House
107 Ebury Street, SW1
Tel: 020-7730 1048
Fax: 020-7730 2574
One of the better basic B&Bs in Victoria, thanks to its long-established, courteous owners. Ask for a quieter room at the rear. Guests have use of a communal kitchen and the courtyard garden. 12 simple rooms (none en suite).

Above: at the National Gallery
Right: city in bloom

ATTRACTIONS

Museum Pass

If you're intending to do a thorough cultural trawl of the capital, the GoSeeCard pass is good value. It provides entry to 17 of London's major attractions and museums (the Imperial War Museum, Science Museum, Museum of London, etc.). A 3-day pass costs £16 (families of two adults and up to four children aged under 16: £32), and a 7-day pass £26 (families £50). The cards are sold at participating museums.

Tours and Walks

Several companies run open-top bus tours around central London. There isn't much to choose between them, except that the commentary on some is live, and on others it is recorded. Tours take around 90 minutes, but you can hop on and off at various stops on the way. Main starting points include Piccadilly Circus and Trafalgar Square, and tickets cost around £12. You might also consider a tour in a black cab, which at £65 for two hours is hardly more expensive if you fill the taxi with five passengers – and you can get the cabbie to tailor the tour to where you want to go. Call Black Taxi Tours of London on 020-7289 4371.

Many companies offer interesting walks around London – some themed, some focused on particular parts of the city. The long-established Original London Walks (020-7624 3978) has an enormous repertoire of walks, from pub crawls to a tour of the National Gallery, and walks round the haunts of Jack the Ripper and The Beatles.

USEFUL NUMBERS

Airports

Gatwick: 01293 535 353
Heathrow: 020-8759 4321
London City: 020 7646 0000
Luton: 01582 405 100
Stansted: 01279 680 500

Airlines

Aer Lingus: 0645 737 747
Air Canada: 0990 247 226
Air France: 020-8742 6600

Air India: 020-7495 7950
Alitalia: 020-7602 7111
American Airlines: 0345 789 789
British Airways: 0345 222 111
British Midland: 0345 554 554
Cathay Pacific: 020-7747 8888
Continental Airlines: 0800 776 464
Delta Airlines: 0800 414 767
Easyjet: 0990 292 929
GO: 0845 605 4321
Iberia: 020-7830 0011
KLM UK: 0870 507 4074
Lufthansa: 0345 737 747
Qantus: 0345 747 767
Ryanair: 0541 569 569
SAA: 020-7312 5000
Sabena: 020-8780 1444
TWA: 0345 333 333
United Airlines: 0845 844 4777
Virgin Atlantic: 01293 747 747

USEFUL ADDRESSES

Embassies/High Commissions

Australia: Australia House, Strand, WC2 4LA. Tel: 020-7379 4334
Canada: Macdonald House, 1 Grosvenor Square, W1X 0AB. Tel: 020-7258 6600.
India: India House, Aldwych, WC2B 4NA. Tel: 020-7836 8484.
Ireland: 17 Grosvenor Place, SW1X 7HR. Tel: 020-7235 2171.
Jamaica: 2 Prince Consort Road, SW7 2BZ. Tel: 020-7823 9911.
New Zealand: 80 Haymarket, SW1Y 4TQ. Tel: 020-7930 8422.
South Africa: South Africa House, Trafalgar Square, WC2N 5DP. Tel: 020-7451 7299.
United States: 24 Grosvenor Square, W1A 1AE. Tel: 020 7499 9000.

FURTHER READING

Clout, Hugh (ed), *The Times London History Atlas*. Times Books. Detailed maps and plans illuminate the development of the city, with authoritative text and illustrations.
Insight Compact Guide: London. Apa Publications. Practical, easy-to-carry and affordable guide designed for use on the spot.
Insight Guide: London. Apa Publications. A guidebook combining comprehensive destination information with superb pictures and entertaining, insightful essays.
Pepys, Samuel, *The Concise Pepys*. First-hand account of life in 17th-century London, including the Great Fire.
Piper, David, *Artist's London*. Weidenfeld and Nicholson. Fascinating pictures of London throughout its history.
Richardson, John, *London and its People: A Social History*. Barrie and Jenkins. Interesting account of the lives of rich and poor Londoners from the medieval times to the present.
Vansittart, Peter, *A Literary Companion: London*. John Murray. Tour of the haunts of London writers.
Wittich, John, *Discovering London's Parks and Squares*. Shire Publications. A walker's companion.

Also from Insight Guides...

Insight Guides is the classic series, providing the complete picture with expert and informative text and stunning photography. Each book is an ideal travel planner, a reliable on-the-spot companion – and a superb visual souvenir of a trip. 193 titles.

Insight Maps are designed to complement the guidebooks. They provide full mapping of major destinations, and their laminated finish gives them ease of use and durability. 65 titles.

Insight Compact Guides are handy reference books, modestly priced yet comprehensive. The text, pictures and maps are all cross-referenced, making them ideal books to consult while seeing the sights. 119 titles.

INSIGHT POCKET GUIDE TITLES

Aegean Islands
Algarve
Alsace
Amsterdam
Athens
Atlanta
Bahamas
Baja Peninsula
Bali
Bali Bird Walks
Bangkok
Barbados
Barcelona
Bavaria
Beijing
Berlin
Bermuda
Bhutan
Boston
Brisbane & the Gold Coast
British Columbia
Brittany
Brussels
Budapest
California, Northern
Canton
Chiang Mai
Chicago
Corsica
Costa Blanca
Costa Brava
Costa Rica
Crete
Denmark
Fiji Islands
Florence
Florida
Florida Keys
French Riviera (Côte d'Azur)
Gran Canaria
Hawaii
Hong Kong
Hungary
Ibiza
Ireland
Ireland's Southwest
Israel
Istanbul
Jakarta
Jamaica
Kathmandu Bikes & Hikes
Kenya
Kuala Lumpur
Lisbon
Loire Valley
London
Los Angeles
Macau
Madrid
Malacca
Maldives
Mallorca
Malta
Manila
Marbella
Melbourne
Mexico City
Miami
Montreal
Morocco
Moscow
Munich
Nepal
New Delhi
New Orleans
New York City
New Zealand
Oslo and Bergen
Paris
Penang
Perth
Phuket
Prague
Provence
Puerto Rico
Quebec
Rhodes
Rome
Sabah
St. Petersburg
San Francisco
Sarawak
Sardinia
Scotland
Seville, Cordoba & Granada
Seychelles
Sicily
Sikkim
Singapore
Southeast England
Southern Spain
Sri Lanka
Sydney
Tenerife
Thailand
Tibet
Toronto
Tunisia
Turkish Coast
Tuscany
Venice
Vienna
Vietnam
Yogjakarta
Yucatán Peninsula

ACKNOWLEDGEMENTS

11, 23, 30B, 32, 34B, 35, 43B, 44, 45, 49T, 50, 55T, 55B, 57B, 62, 64B, 70, 72, 81, 84, 87, 93, 85	**Apa/LCP**
2/3, 25T, 26B, 30, 36B, 38, 43T, 53, 78, 84, 99	**Apa/Glyn Genin**
51, 52, 62	**Apa/Bill Wassman**
Title, 20 21, 24, 37B, 39, 40B, 49B, 61, 68 74, 79, 80, 87, 88, 90, 91, 94, 95, Back Cover	**Natasha Babaian**
14	**BBC Hulton Picture Library**
Cover	**Joe Cornish/Stone**
83	**Andrew Eames**
12	**Fotomas**
40T	**Tony Halliday**
65	**Blaine Harrington**
47	**Courtesy of Harrods**
60, 75, 77, 97	**Carlotta Junger**
63B	**Neil Menneer**
22, 25B, 28, 29, 33, 34, 36T, 41, 58B, 64T 66B	**Robert Mort**
10, 15	**Courtesy of The Museum of London**
16, 46, 82	**Richard T Nowitz**
63T	**Tony Page**
58T	**Spectrum Colour Library**
69	**Adam Woolfitt**
Cartography	**David Priestley**
Cover Design	**Carlotta Junger**
Production	**Tanvir Virdee**

INDEX